This latest installment of brilliance on leadership has been my North Star on how I lead those around me at work, at home and in society.

—EMMANUEL ACHO

New York Times Bestselling Author and Host of

Uncomfortable Conversations with a Black Man

Donnie Maib exemplifies leadership day in and day out. His secret sauce is inspiring and helpful for all in leadership positions!

—COLT MCCOY

NFL Quarterback, Author

Donnie Maib is a leader of leaders. I've known him since I was 18 years old, but it was what happened after I met him that changed everything. Donnie Maib pushed me past what I thought was possible and helped me to understand what it takes to be an exceptional leader. His selflessness, fearlessness and servants' heart will help transform you and your team. Whether it was national championships or bustling professional careers, Donnie Maib was the brain behind it all. I can't wait for you to check this book out and learn what I learned. The leadership isn't always easy, but it's always worth it.

—SAM ACHO

Author, Motivational Speaker, ESPN Analyst

Coach Maib combines tested leadership methods with strategies gleaned from his unique experience at the highest echelon of sports. *The Secret Sauce of Leadership* is required reading for anyone who is committed to elevating their capacity to lead others.

—DARON K. ROBERTS

Coach, Author, and Speaker

As a two-time National Championship coach, understanding and implementing leadership strategies are key components to developing individual and team success. Donnie is a master leadership coach, who I lean on daily, to help me, my captains and team grow. As a coach, I must know the way so I can develop and show my athletes the way these principles are staples to our championship program.

—JERRITT ELLIOTT
Volleyball Head Coach, University of Texas

Donnie is an incredible coach, motivator, and leader! He has made a huge impact on our leadership program we developed in our company and his message translates from the court to the board room, to the family dinner table! Not only that, but he's an incredible guy with a passion to help others succeed. His down to earth, fun, and relatable style makes his leadership's principles truly enjoyable to learn. Thank you, Donnie, for all that you have taught myself and our team!

—ALLY DAVIDSON
Founder & CEO of Camp Gladiator

In all my life no one has had as profound an impact on my life as a Coach, husband, father, and man than Donnie Maib! I shared an office with Donnie for many years and it was truly a blessing. The lessons learned from him not only in countless conversations but also by his living out his leadership lessons daily. Donnie is a servant leader with a warrior's heart! A compassionate soul whose spirit blazes with passion! Truly a man for all seasons whose leadership style is one that is relational, genuine and can reach anyone right where they are. This book is a must have for coaches, business owners, parents, anyone who has people that look to them for leadership and guidance this is the one. I know 1st hand the impact that Donnie had and has on me and my family. Truly a blessing to all he touches. I'm proud of the work he has put into this book. You will be moved. I'm also honored to call him a friend and a brother.

—COACH TIM CROSS
Veteran Football Coach

I've known Donnie Maib for years and everyone that has been around him as an athlete-coach and coworker says the same thing, he's an even better person and in this book, you'll see why he is so beloved and respected by so many across a vast landscape. Coach Maib lays out how to lead and elevate others around you, how to be the defining force in someone's life and to help them become the best version of themselves.

—MATT DURANT
Head Strength & Conditioning Coach, University of La Verne

I have worked with Donnie for over seventeen years with champion athletes at Texas, so I have seen firsthand his exemplary work as a high-performance coach and leadership mentor. Fortunately, he has included these best practices in *The Secret Sauce of Leadership*. Now, you can learn what the Longhorns do about transformative leadership principles and practices, from Coach D himself.

—DR. MIKE VOIGHT
Author, Leadership Consultant, Professor Physical Education and Human Performance Central Connecticut State University

Donnie Maib is no stranger to the subject of leadership. As a Director of Olympic Sports Athletic Performance, he has taken his teams to great heights competitively as well as teaching young leaders how to win, lose, and lead others. He not only molded leaders, but he is also a terrific teacher on leadership. Most of all he is a stellar model of what a great leader looks and acts like. If you are needing a refresher on leadership, this is a book you need to read, as does your team. It is practical and provides depth and what it means to lead from the heart and with strength of character.

—DEBORAH LEVERETT
Enterra-Partners President

Donnie Maib has channeled more than three decades of experience to write a timely and relevant book that every current and emerging leader should read. Powerful and practical, Donnie shares insight on his journey to success and provides his keys to becoming an extraordinary leader. Everyone's recipe for success should include his "Secret Sauce!"

—ALLEN HARDIN

Chief Medical Officer, The University of Texas

One of my favorite people and an elite leader, Donnie Maib delivers with his new book *The Secret Sauce of Leadership*. Donnie has the unique ability to take high level leadership principles and make them stick with his down to earth humility and humor. Do yourself, your family, and your organization a favor and grab this resource as fast as you can.

—RON MCKEEFERY, MA, MSCC, RSCC*E

The University of Alabama

Collegiate Strength and Conditioning Coach of the Year (2008) (2016)

International Coach of the Year (2020)

THE TWO BUCKETS OF *leadership*

DONNIE MAIB

ISBN 979-8-9890672-2-0 (Paperback)
ISBN 979-8-9890672-4-4 (Hardcover)
ISBN 979-8-9890672-3-7 (eBook)

DEDICATION

To my family who have supported and encouraged me through the years and helped me become a better leader. To my amazing wife Karen. You have always been my biggest cheerleader, always had my back, and stood in my corner no matter what. Thank you babe. I love you! To my beautiful daughters Isabel, Anna, Evelyn, and Olivia. You have not only made me a proud dad, you have inspired me to never stop growing and learning. The greatest title I was ever given is to be your dad. Thank you for being such a blessing!

CONTENTS

INTRODUCTION
Carrying Buckets

W hen I was growing up, we owned several wild horses. We lived on five acres of land in Tennessee, and since we had no source of water, those horses required a lot of care. As the only boy in the family, I was my dad's sidekick for horse care. One cold winter, the temperature dropped well below freezing that night and all the water buckets froze solid. My dad called for me, "Son, we have a problem. The horses don't have any other option for water. If we don't get them water soon, they will start to dehydrate, and we will have a bigger issue on our hands. Go get two buckets from the shed and fill them up from the tap in the house and carry them to the horses." A simple enough request. Did I mention the horses were wild? If you know anything about wild horses, they spook easily. Each time I filled up the five-gallon buckets and lugged them out to the horses, they ran from me not knowing what I was doing. I must have carried those buckets a country mile to care for those horses that day. Eventually they settled down and realized what I had in the buckets – water to save their lives!

Every person in leadership is like me that day: they carry two buckets. The only difference is one bucket holds "water" and the other holds "gasoline". Depending on the situation, person, and circumstance a leader uses one bucket or the other, or a combination of the two. Water cools, cleanses, refreshes, quenches, dampens and damages. Gas, on the other hand, can be explosive, toxic, destructive or it can fuel and propel you. The outcome you are looking for determines which bucket you use. Great leaders not only understand this, but have discernment and wisdom about which bucket to use in any given situation. Over the years I have seen situations get out of control because the leader added fuel to the fire by using their words poorly or making decisions without seeking counsel. I have also witnessed leaders tactfully and carefully weigh their actions and, like a master firefighter, bring calm to the most explosive situations. What could have turned into a disastrous scenario ended up being no problem at all.

For the past thirty years, I have had the privilege of working alongside some of the best coaches, teams and leaders in the world. From Coach of the year award winners to Olympic gold medalists, National Champions or record breaking Heisman trophy winners, one thing has helped these high performers standout: leadership. In my previous book, *the Secret Sauce of Leadership* we talked about the little nuances to help you move from ordinary to extraordinary. In this book, I will continue to draw from my experience and the insights I have gleaned over the years and will address more difficult and challenging aspects of being a leader: casting vision, leading staff, hiring, firing, and promotions. Anything not handled with care can cause stressful problems, complicate relationships, and cost you credibility as a leader. We will delve into some simple ways to improve your leadership acumen, and offer practical insight and understanding on which proverbial bucket to use.

I will discuss different aspects of leadership throughout this book. How you apply the principles of the two buckets will be determined by your desired outcome. Each leader approaches a given circumstance in a unique way. Leadership is an art. Outcomes are determined by many variables, and your leadership will steer the way toward success or failure. At the end of the day, you may not be carrying water to save horses, but you are caring for people. Leadership is about people. You may not have the most resources, the best circumstances, or support you need to lead right now, but you are the leader and you are responsible. Using the right bucket at the right time, with the right people, at the right place will lead to greater success in the long run. Choose your bucket wisely.

CHAPTER 1

Begin with the End in Mind

"Don't despise these small beginnings."

Zechariah 4:10

"I want you there at 6 am to watch the women's basketball team workout." This was one of the early assignments E.J. "Doc" Kreis gave me. My only task was to sit on the sideline and observe the workout session. Just watch. No coaching or leading the team through any of the workout. The head women's basketball coach for the Colorado Buffaloes was Ceal Barry, a tough, disciplined, intense, and very successful coach who had lost faith in the weight room. She pulled her players out of the weight room and led all team workouts for the off-season. I was sent to watch. I was so confused. I didn't sign up for this – I wanted to coach! Like a good soldier though, I showed up and observed. Over time, I noticed something happening. The team liked me being there. Though I didn't understand why and didn't like getting up at o'dark thirty, I began to look forward to seeing the team and began encouraging and cheering them on in their workouts. I gave more high fives to those women during those weeks than I had ever given my entire life.

Something else was also happening. Coach Barry was watching *me.* She observed how the team worked harder with my support and encouragement. Though she never said two words to me over that time, she saw the influence I was having. I will never forget the day Coach Barry walked up to me, looked intently into my eyes and said, "You have them for the next six weeks. I want to see what you can do with the team". I was dumbfounded and barely managed a stunned "Yes, ma'am!" For the next six weeks I trained the women's basketball team and had a blast! By daily doing a seemingly insignificant task of showing up and encouraging others, I was given the chance to coach. What seemed like a waste of time led to a big opportunity. In hindsight, I can see how seemingly meaningless jobs impacted my entire career. Never dismiss a small beginning.

There are only two jobs where you start out at the top: grave digging and ditch digging. All other jobs begin at the bottom and you work your way up. This is both the greatest and worst thing about being a leader. Some of the most insignificant opportunities have turned into the coolest, most rewarding outcomes over time. These days everyone wants to excel quickly and enjoy every assignment they are given. Unfortunately, life doesn't work that way.

Big oak trees were once a seed. They were tiny objects nobody noticed. Once planted and nurtured and given plenty of sunlight, they grew. Over time the seed became a massive immovable oak tree. That's a great analogy to our career path. Careers take time. We have to keep working at it. If we cannot do a great job with small opportunities, we will not do a great job with bigger opportunities.

When I first started out in coaching, I didn't get to coach. I ran errands, hung signs, scraped rust off the floor, painted bumper plates, checked roll, filled Gatorade machines, picked up messes I didn't make, made airport pick-ups and drop offs, and the list goes on. Small beginnings are never glamorous or fun. Most of the time no one even notices what you are doing unless you don't do it. Even though menial tasks are small, they are actions that, if left undone, will eventually create big problems. When starting out, take great care to do small things with excellence. Starting small doesn't mean you are small. I really struggled with this early on: my pride kept telling me, "You played football at the University of Georgia, and this is what you went to school for?" My ego took a massive hit, and yet it was the best thing for me.

When first starting out in a career, it is not unusual to find out that you may actually decline before you go up in your career path. It's called the Sigmoid Curve. Whenever you start out in something new, you have no base to launch from and you actually take a dip first. (see fig. 1.1) Over time, if you stick with it, you will start to climb and move up.

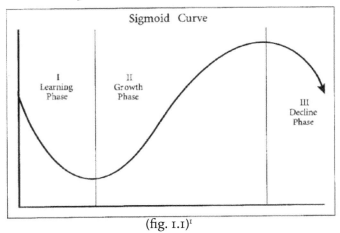

(fig. 1.1)[1]

We don't want to deal with small beginnings; we want to start out near the top and move up quickly, with minimal resistance. We live in a microwave society. We can access and download powerful information in seconds, but careers don't work like that. Career growth takes time.

Here are some benefits to starting small and taking time:

1. **Maturity** - Maturity doesn't always come with age and experience, but without it you may not keep your job for long and your influence will be limited. Maturity is a slow process, during which you grow up and realize it's not all about you. If you want to be seen as a leader, you will need maturity and selflessness.

2. **Perspective** - How you view situations and choose to react to crises will determine your leadership effectiveness. When you start small, your perspective is small simply because you haven't done the job long enough. As you persevere, navigating good times and bad, your perspective will change. As your perspective changes, you will become more equipped to lead and your capacity to handle multi-faceted situations will increase.

3. **Humility** - Arrogance is not a healthy attribute in a leader. Rapid promotion makes you susceptible to arrogance. You may find yourself thinking you are far more important than you really are. We are all replaceable. Slow growth and gradual promotion will help keep you humble. Humility helps you remain grounded and increases your chances of keeping your job or role.

4. **Competence** - Practice leads to competence. When I first started teaching Olympic lifts, I was horrible. Early on, I addressed

my lack of competence through working camps and small groups. My skills increased slowly over time and, without even realizing it, I became a strong teacher, with an eye for technical problems.

5.   **Flops** – One of the key benefits of starting small and going slow is learning what you aren't very good at. Though this may seem like a waste, it will provide great value when leading. When you become aware of areas where you are weak and are lacking in ability, you will build a team around you that is gifted where you aren't as competent. Part of leading is bringing together a team of individuals that are not only gifted in what they do, but they also find great satisfaction in working collaboratively.

It is no wonder that one of my favorite sayings is this: "Don't despise the day of small beginnings". In other words, when you are first starting out, don't jump too soon and hate it. Give it some time and keep at it. Don't look down on small opportunities with disdain, but take those insignificant responsibilities and apply yourself to them. It will lead to bigger and better tasks. Doing an excellent job with a small task almost always leads to recognition and more responsibility. Though it may take time, you will look back and will be amazed with how far you have come. You will be well on your way to being a leader.

Leave It Better Than You Found It

After months of house hunting, we finally moved into our first house in November 2000. It was an older home built in 1984, and the previous owners had done some light refurbishing prior to selling. There were new wood floors in the kitchen and living room and though the floors made the home look a little better, there was still a lot of work to do. I was ecstatic to be a new homeowner, and up for the challenge.

I will never forget my first DIY project. My family and I had returned home from church one Sunday morning and I happened to walk out into our empty garage. I noticed a nice sized pool of water in the center of the floor. I looked up at the ceiling and all the surrounding walls and saw no water leakage. Being a new homeowner I called a good friend who works in construction and shared my dilemma. Immediately he grew serious and he told me to check the water heater.

"Check what?" I asked. I had no clue what a water heater was or where I might find one in my house. With some guidance, I located it in a small closet in the garage. My friend instructed me to locate the installation sticker on the side of the heater, to see what year the unit was installed. Turns out, it was the original water heater installed when the house was built in 1984. I owned a 16 year old water heater, and it was in its last moments of life! My friend hung up and immediately came over.

We hustled to Home Depot, where I purchased my first brand new hot water heater. My friend inspected the old water heater and discovered it was so old the metal was rusted through and you could push through the metal like a piece of wet paper. It was a miracle it had not leaked all 40 gallons of water into my garage. For the next six hours my friend helped install our new water heater. Disaster diverted! I was thankful that I had a friend with the skill set to help me in the situation. This experience was a huge lesson and taught me a valuable lesson of new home ownership: leave it better than you found it!

As leaders, this principle is very applicable. We are often given opportunities that are not glamorous. We accept new positions with excitement, hope, and enthusiasm. The sky's the limit and we have confidence we can turn it around and make it better. It doesn't take long to realize we have inherited problems we didn't create, we uncovered issues we have no idea how to navigate or handle, and find ourselves with levels of frustration we did not anticipate. We need what I received when I found that puddle of water in my garage: a reality check. We need to consider the bigger picture. The reality is becoming a leader will take longer than you thought, be harder than you imagined, and will require far more help than you anticipated.

Your primary objective with any new position is this: Leave it better than you found it. If you want to lead, it is imperative you think differently. Don't just consider your job individually, but strive to see the bigger picture. Perhaps your position hasn't had a good relational history with other staff or departments. Perhaps your predecessor neglected an aspect of their job that reflected negatively on the department and you need to address it. On the other hand, perhaps your position has experienced high turnover rates and lacks stability. Maybe your initial goal is to increase pay rates to levels that create stability for you and others. Each of these require a different set of skills as a leader. Early in my career we had an intern who started out as a volunteer and worked his way into a part time paid position. Eventually he was rewarded with a full time position. How did he do it? He took the initiative to notice problems and, without anyone telling him, developed and implemented solutions. He wrote a computer program that allowed us to print out daily workouts for athletes, and he took our most unorganized closet, drew up a plan for shelving to keep it organized. I was so sure he was wasting his time and kissing up to our boss. Man, was I wrong! His initiative paid off, paving the way for promotion after promotion at other schools. He left it better than he found it. In doing so, he increased his value and importance.

What are some ways you can leave your job or position better than you found it? Here are some ideas to consider:

1. **Identify the Pain Points** - What can be improved or solved to impact and help a lot of people? What would improve how everyone does their job? Can you take on a task everyone hates to make everyone's job easier? Have a discussion with your boss and make a plan before taking it on.

2. **Does Your Employer Have an Internship Program?** If so, can you contribute? How can you get involved? Is there an onboarding process or some educational sessions you can help serve with? Are there any materials that need preparing in advance? Volunteering to help with jobs that others don't want to do or maybe don't have the margin to invest in right now can be a small opportunity for you to get involved. Finding ways to improve even the smallest of tasks goes a long way.

3. **Are There Any Paperwork Duties You Could Take Off Someone's Hands?** Remember, sometimes you will get the best one-on-one time by serving others in higher positions. Don't use the opportunity to wear them out and ask a bunch of questions. Just do your job with excellence and follow through. Over time, you will earn the respect and trust of that individual that will qualify you to ask questions.

4. **Are There Any Work Events You Can Help Plan and Oversee?** Early in my career, I frequently worked camps. Football camps,

strength camps, etc. It is grueling work, but the experience gained helped prepare me for leadership. You have to hire, fire, deal with angry parents, set pay scales, formulate policies, negotiate with consultants, organize daily schedules, deal with crisis, loss, fatigue, burnout, and a host of other fun things! Never forget that leadership development grows through being uncomfortable in difficult situations. Though it is not always fun, the return on investment is well worth the discomfort you undergo to grow as a leader.

5. **Non-Profit Organizations** – If your job doesn't have the opportunities you are looking for, think outside the box. What other interests or passions do you have? Is there an organization or non-profit you can get involved with? If you can lead a group of volunteers who do not follow you because of a paycheck, you will be able to lead anyone. Some of the best training, experience, and leadership development hasn't happened in my job. I have found it outside the four walls of my job. The challenge will be finding the energy and hours to donate. You may not have excess free time, but make it a priority to look for different opportunities to serve and find something that interests you. Not only will it get you out of your comfort zone, but the experience alone will change your life and make you a better leader!

We lived in our first home for eleven years, undertaking numerous improvement projects. We installed new kitchen countertops, sinks, lights, and doors; we painted inside and out, erected new fences, hung ceiling fans, and the list goes on. Each project was challenging but in the end, the resale value of the home doubled. We left it better than we found it!

Will you leave your job better than you found it? Will the person coming after you in your current job, role, or position benefit from your hard work and passion? Or will you hold back because it's not your dream job? Will you not do your best because it's not a visible role? As a leader, leave your position better than you found it. No matter if you get what you want or you make the progress you were striving to reach, do it anyway. It may not always go the way you wanted or happen as fast as you were hoping for, but do it anyway. You may not get the credit and recognition you deserve but do it anyway. Years ago I read the poem below by Mother Teresa that helped me keep the right focus and attitude to ensure I would leave it better than I found it.

Anyway
by Mother Teresa[2]

People are often unreasonable, illogical and self-centered;
Forgive them anyway.

If you are kind, people may accuse you of selfish, ulterior motives;
Be kind anyway.

If you are successful, you will win some false friends and some true enemies;
Succeed anyway.

If you are honest and frank, people may cheat you;
Be honest and frank anyway.

What you spend years building, someone could destroy overnight;
Build anyway.

If you find serenity and happiness, they may be jealous;
Be happy anyway.

The good you do today, people will often forget tomorrow;
Do good anyway.

Give the world the best you have, and it may never be enough;
Give the world the best you've got anyway.

You see, in the final analysis, it is between you and your God;
It was never between you and them anyway.

—

Be the Employee You Would Hire

Perspective changes everything. I don't remember exactly when it happened, but early in my coaching career I had an 'aha' moment. At the time, I was getting sick of my boss telling me what to do. The cycle was always the same: receiving an order for some menial task anybody could do but then refusing to do it. I dragged my feet and put the task off until my boss reminded me again and again, or eventually asked someone else to take care of it.

And then it hit me: one day I hoped to be a director and lead a staff. As a director, how would I feel about my performance? I was not completing tasks or following through. I was walking around with a sour attitude, and not being someone my boss could count on. It was a sobering moment to realize I would not have hired me as my own employee. That breakthrough led to a new pattern of thinking and behavior. I altered my perspective and got to work, taking pride in my work in order to be a coach I would one day want to hire.

I viewed my work in a whole new light. What was drudgery suddenly had a new purpose and meaning. What I had brushed over and oftentimes completed half-heartedly became opportunities to raise the bar of excellence. Over time, I became someone people could count on. Slowly but surely I became a leader without realizing it. I became a coach who stood out and set myself apart by how I did my job. Instead of doing the bare minimum, I took on small extras. Mahatma Gandhi said "Be the change you wish to see in the world"[3]. Anyone can complain and point out problems, but it takes a leader to step up and do something about it. John C. Maxwell says it best: "It's easier to belch up the bologna, than it is to bring home the bacon"[4]. In other words, a good future leader knows you need to begin by acting like the assistant you would want to hire. A willingness to change your perspective and adjust your attitude will radically transform how you do your job. Here are some ideas to help you get started:

1. **Be Proactive** - Sitting back and always waiting for someone to tell you what to do will not do you any good. Being the type of employee that is looking for ways to be productive shows you are not only engaged in your work, but also that you want to be there. Pay attention to how things are done around you. Is there anything you can do to help prepare for the day ahead for a coworker? Have you noticed ways to help make work flow more efficient? Are there any areas that need organizing better? Small actions, if taken initiative early on, can make a big impression.

2. **Fill a Gap** – Learning how your boss thinks and paying attention to what they like or dislike will pay dividends. A boss who

might be disorganized or incompetent in a certain area can provide an opportunity for you to step up and fill in a gap to shore up a weakness. In doing so, you will learn new skills and gain new perspectives you wouldn't have otherwise.

3. **Pick Up the Trash** - One small thing you can do consistently is pick up the trash in your area, or someone else's. You might be thinking, 'I didn't drop it there' and you are correct. Though you didn't litter, you can still collect it. It's the difference between having a renter's mentality versus an owner's mentality. Those who rent rarely take good care of what they are using. Owners, on the other hand, take great care with what they own, wanting it to last for a long time. I have learned that if nobody takes ownership then trash doesn't get picked up. I decided long ago that when I see trash on the ground, I pick it up and place it in the trash can. Why? I want to take pride in not only *how* I work but *where* I work.

4. **Lift, Don't Lean** - Be the person who lightens the load. Look for those who could use help, and offer to assist. Be a servant of others. In doing so, you send the message to others you not only care about your work, but you care about those you work with.

5. **Prepare for the Future** - As you change your perspective, one other thing you can do is visualize the position you want. Are there gaps in your skills? Start taking classes, learning, and studying now. Signing up for leadership or managerial courses and inconvenience yourself on weekends or nights. Ask someone to mentor you in an area you want to see growth. Step up and ask for more responsibility to stretch you personally

and professionally. Preparing for the future isn't always fun or easy, but you will be better equipped to lead because you have done the work.

CHAPTER 2

Charting Your Course

"Anyone can steer the ship; it takes a leader to chart the course."

John C. Maxwell

Snow Blind

Snowstorms are treacherous. When I was living in Colorado, I was driving back from a friend's house when a blizzard-like snowstorm hit on my route home. Snow began dumping out of the sky in sheets so thick I couldn't see two inches in front of my truck. In that instance, I realized what the term "snow blind" meant. It was dark, and the light from my headlights were reflecting on the white snow as it fell and bouncing back into my eyes. Not knowing what to do, I pulled over to the side of the road to try and get my bearings. I couldn't see the road in front of me and was concerned that if I continued driving, I would run the risk of driving off a cliff, since I was in the mountains. So I sat there, stunned, not sure what to do next. In my mind, I began to consider the idea of spending the night in my car stuck on the side of the road, but as I sat there contemplating my next steps, a car drove by. It was at that moment that I realized that I was the only car that had stopped. Though there weren't many cars on the road that night, the snow didn't stop them from driving. These other cars had slowed down, but continued to drive even in the heavy downpour of snow. I then began to notice that everyone had turned off their main headlights and were driving with only their low beam lights turned on. I reached down and turned off my main headlights and surprisingly, I could see again! I slowly entered back onto the road and drove for the next several miles until I had made it through the worst part of the storm. Once I made it out of the thick snowfall, I was able to turn my main headlights back on and made it safely home.

I share that story because leaders need vision. Leadership isn't just about perks, positions, and people. At its bare essence, leadership is about being a difference-maker. There is something in the world that is not right, and you, the leader, see a way to make it better. Sometimes it can be something small like reorganizing a part of your daily workflow to increase productivity. Other times it can be something much larger like restructuring an entire department so different people can be aligned to work closer together to accomplish the mission, or it could be painting an innovative picture to solve a cash flow problem for your business that is outside the norm. No matter what level of leadership you attain to reach, now, and in the future, you must have vision. President John Fitzgerald Kennedy completely changed the course of space travel when he shared his vision of putting a man on the moon. His vision was something completely unheard of and didn't seem possible. It was a ludicrous idea. However, because he had a vision of what could be, he was able to paint a picture of the future. Before the technology even existed to make it a reality, he could envision how it would help the US lead the world in space travel and put the first-ever man on the moon. Not only did he have a vision, but he also put money, resources, and research towards the NASA program and turned it into a reality. It didn't happen overnight, it cost billions of dollars and man hours, and there were a lot of obstacles along the way, but if there wasn't a vision, it would have never transpired. The unthinkable came to life and it all started with a vision.

Let's look at five components of vision you will need as a leader if you want to make a difference:

1. **Compelling** – If your vision doesn't get people excited, give them hope, or help them see what might be, they will not act. Chuck Yeager broke the sound barrier on October 14th, 1947. The actual event happened in a day, but it took a team of scientists along with years of research and development to accomplish this feat.[5] Years prior many people had come very close to breaking the barrier but the technology didn't exist. During that time, many believed supersonic flight was impossible and that an "invisible" barrier in the sky would destroy the aircraft. Earlier failed attempts leading up to that day threatened the success of the program. After some upgrades to the stabilizers on the wings, Chuck Yeager made the leap into supersonic flight, shattering the sound barrier. He became the first human to travel faster than the speed of sound. What seemed like it would never happen came to fruition. Having a dream and a vision was what helped them to keep searching to find a way. It stirred excitement, created buzz, and got people thinking creatively. If you are struggling

with people to get moving, it could be the lack of a compelling vision. When a vision captures people's hearts and stirs their souls, something special starts to happen. They are pulled, not pushed. They become motivated, not manipulated. They stop hitting the snooze button forty-seven times in the morning before getting out of bed. When a vision is compelling, it answers the question 'What might be?' It tears down barriers and breaks the glass ceiling holding you back. No more of the 'same old, same old'.

2. **Challenging** – A great vision is challenging. It kicks against the status quo. It's not always certain and it definitely isn't easy. Oftentimes it will seem out of reach and impossible. Accomplishing your vision will require you to change and to grow. You will have to step out of your comfort zone. You may lack the skills, resources, and support before you even start, but you will be able to make it happen as you step out. If your vision is too easy it won't stretch people. If it's too hard, it may dissuade or discourage others. Seek to strike a balance and find the right mix of being far enough out of reach that people believe it is possible, but not so far that it discourages them. My dad used to send me this quote when I was struggling with vision: "Make no small plans, for they have no power to stir the soul"[6]. As you cast your vision, let it challenge people and invite them to a higher level.

3. **Collaborative** – If you can accomplish your vision on your own, it is too small. The bigger the vision, the more people required to make it happen. The more people involved, the greater the chance of friction. As contrary as it seems, many

leaders struggle to achieve a large vision when everyone is too cooperative. If there is no push back or input on how the vision can be reached, you often miss valuable ideas that could help get you to the end goal. However, when you have a big vision, and a large group of people are involved it needs to be collaborative. There is a difference between being cooperative and collaborative. John Maxwell says "Cooperation is working together agreeably, collaboration is working together aggressively."[7] Everyone isn't always agreeable. Disney's Pixar studio has a "brain trust"[8] which is a group of people who, in the early stages of the film and story line development, allow for pushback from staff on what could be changed to improve the film. In those meetings, emotions ran hot, disagreements happened, and tension occurred. If they didn't collaborate and work together the movies still might have happened but the vision Ed Catmull had for Pixar would not have come to pass.

4. **Clarity** – A vision paints a picture. The clearer the picture the better. If a leader is unable to provide clarity to their vision, it will be foggy in the hearts and minds of the followers. One of my all-time favorite sayings is "Write the vision down, make it plain on tablets so those who read it will run" Habakkuk 2:2[9]. In essence, if you want people to act, the vision better be clear. Loss of clarity equals loss of buy in. If your vision lacks clarity, go back and refine it. Get feedback and ask others if there is any part of the vision that is confusing, uncertain, or fuzzy. Is it too far reaching, not specific enough, or unclear on what you are trying to accomplish? Does it need to be dialed in, polished, and adjusted? Are the people able to envision

how it will come to pass? Be sure to use words, metaphors, analogies, illustrations, and stories to add clarity. When I was in college, I took some art classes, and often my drawings and paintings would have areas that weren't clear. There would be some part of the images that seemed off. I went back and worked on those areas that were not clear, and my painting came alive. It is the same with vision, if the images seem fuzzy or out of focus, go back and add some clarity.

5. **Continuous** – Andy Stanley says, "Vision leaks"[10]. Any vision intended to make a difference needs to be continuously shared. If you fail to refresh your vision, it will be forgotten. Remind others of it often. Be creative on how you accomplish this. Create banners, t-shirts, coffee mugs, quarterly themes, wristbands, branding, and events that remind people what you are reaching for. Find ways to measure the vision. Don't just assume everyone understands because you created some social media posts and sent out a few emails. Protect the vision by consistently bringing it up in the hearts and minds of your followers. As you do this, the vision will start to become a reality. It will no longer be just 'your' vision but 'our' vision. When you get to the point where you feel like you are talking about the vision too much, you are in the right spot. If there is one thing I have seen, it is leaders not understanding how a vision leaks. Vision leaks when you fail to revisit or talk about the main mission you are on. The longer you go without recasting the vision, the easier it is for people to lose motivation on the way to attaining it. If you are having trouble accomplishing your vision, ask yourself 'where is it leaking at'? When was the

last time you met with your team about the vision? Are they aware of how they are doing? How much progress has the team made so far? Are they close to their goal? What challenges are holding them back or slowing you down? Has morale dropped off? Sometimes even a short meeting every few weeks with an update can keep people fired up and raring to go.

It has been many years since I was snow blind on the side of the road in the middle of nowhere Colorado, but I will never forget the lesson that night. If you can't see where you are going you might run off the road and wreck, wander onto the wrong path, or completely stop to find your bearings. To get my vision back that night, I had to turn off my lights. The snow had blinded me, and it was paralyzing. I had no idea what to do. I was stuck. Until I turned my lights off, I couldn't see clearly.

You may need to do the same. Sometimes we get so busy, stressed out, and discouraged and we lose our vision. The pressures and problems of the work blind us. We wander onto the wrong path, get lost or derailed. My encouragement to you is simple: turn off the lights. Get alone, take time to reflect, dream; go on a retreat or schedule a visit to a company whose staff not only have vision but are accomplishing great things. Make this a regular priority. Vision isn't something leaders need occasionally; it is mission critical when it comes to leading others.

Strategic Planning

Growing up in a large, blended family, we would often take summer vacations together. This typically meant all eight of us would pile into the 1977 Oldsmobile station wagon. It had fake wood paneling and was about as long as a city block. We didn't always have much money for vacation, so we usually chose places within driving distance of Tennessee. On one particular trip to Pensacola, Florida with its beautiful beaches and ocean waves, I showed up with nothing packed. No shoes, no extra clothes, swimsuits, toiletries, or sunscreen. I was completely unprepared. I can still hear my dad asking my stepmom where my shoes were when we got out of the car that day. She was flabbergasted when she realized all my shoes were at home and that I had packed nothing, not even a clean pair of underwear. The mood of excitement upon our arrival immediately had changed to frustration and panic because now we would need to go to the store and purchase all the items I would need during our stay. I cannot recall anything we did that summer in Florida, but I will never forget how not planning and not packing negatively impacted the entire family. Thankfully we didn't have to turn around and go back home, but the money and time we could have spent on fun activities together had to be used to purchase clothes and shoes so I didn't walk around naked and barefoot.

"If you fail to plan you're planning to fail."[11] Benjamin Franklin's adage remains true. As a leader, you will need a plan. If you don't intentionally and regularly think about what you want to accomplish and how you intend to do so, you set yourself up for failure. Many leaders today simply wing it. They don't plan out anything. They lead and manage the day-to-day crises, problems, and pressures, and because they fail to look to the future and see what is coming at them, they are often caught off guard. Their leadership becomes reactive and when a leader is reactive, everyone feels it. Leaders who are more reactive will apply pressure on others due to their lack of foresight.

Proactive leadership, on the other hand, lives in the present, but looks to the future. They anticipate problems, shortages, and changes and make adjustments to accommodate. Problems and pressures still arise but are managed differently because a plan is in place.

If you look in nature, animals innately know when winter is coming. They don't wait for the first snowflake to begin gathering food. They gather food when it is in abundance and begin storing up for winter so that when winter arrives, they don't starve. Instead of dying, they are thriving. This is a picture of proactive planning.

As you continue to chart your course as a leader, let's look at five principles of strategic planning to help you lead:

1. **Schedule Time to Meet** – As simple as it sounds, this is the hardest step. You must set a date and block of time on your calendar with your team to meet and discuss. When you do this, take into consideration the place, the time of day, time of year, and other pressing needs you and your staff may be facing. From my experience, it is essential to remove as many distractions as possible during this time to allow for brainstorming, creative discussion, and taking notes. Find a place separate from the normal workday environment where endless interruptions can hinder your productivity.

2. **Set Some Ground Rules** – Once you have a time, place, and space set some ground rules. No phone zones are required if you want to get the most of your time together. Because you are planning, it will require reflection and uninterrupted thought. One way to do this is to set blocks of time with breaks to allow for using the restroom, checking email, and replying to text messages that might be top of mind. We live in an

overconnected world, and asking your people to go completely off the grid for an extended period is challenging. However, asking people to focus intently for short periods of time is not only doable, but can be very effective and fruitful.

3. **Create an Agenda** – If you want to get a lot done during strategic planning sessions, send out an agenda ahead of time. This works well because you are setting the tone and expectation for your time together. I would recommend putting time limits and emphasis on each time block on the agenda. You may not stick to it exactly, but it gives you some boundaries to work within. Another helpful element you can add is a theme for your meeting. "Creating an Edge", "Finding Our Voice", and "Poke the Box" are themes I have used in the past. Setting a theme not only helped us focus as a team, but also created a sense of excitement with a higher purpose and objective for the coming season. The sooner you can create the agenda and send it out for others to review and prepare their thoughts, the more primed and ready your team will be for discussion. If you send it out last minute, it can potentially bog down your meeting together because they are just seeing it for the first time.

4. **Designate a Notetaker** – Planning always involves coming up with a lot of different ideas, concepts, and thoughts from your staff. I would highly recommend designating someone to capture all the ideas shared as you talk through your agenda. Since this is a planning meeting and nothing is set in stone, consider using big sticky notes you can place on a wall for everyone to see. This allows everyone to think aloud and see what has already been said. Creativity can be contagious and

when you get a room of people together thinking and dreaming big, it can have a profound effect. Once the meeting is over, ask the notetaker to type up all the ideas from the large sticky notes and transfer them to a Word document to be sent out to everyone in the meeting. As the notetaker compiles everything, have them capture any themes that seem to repeat themselves and place them at the top of the document. When a theme is consistently mentioned, that is usually an idea or concern on your team's mind and can be a focus of your planning.

5. **Follow Up and Implement** – Once you have met as a team and come up with a plan, your next step will be to follow up and begin to implement it. There are several practical ways you can do this: assign different parts of the plan to individual staff members with dates to get things done. If you do this, be sure to schedule time to follow up and check on their progress. Another way you can do this, is when you have regular staff meetings throughout the year block out a portion of your meeting to check in on the progress and status of your strategic plan. This holds people accountable as a group and allows for discussion on any challenges or sticking points people are facing on moving the needle on their part of the plan. Lastly, you can meet with people individually to check in on how they are doing and if they need assistance. Over the years, I have used all types of methods and strategies and each one of them works depending on how large the scope of the plan, taking into consideration who is involved, and what timeline you are working on. Use a method and strategy you and your team can agree upon.

We still go on vacations now that I am much older, and I am way better at planning than I was back then. I still forget things, and overpack at times, but it is better vacationing with a plan than spontaneously hopping in the car and arriving unprepared. As you work to lay out your strategic plan as a leader, here are some questions you will want to consider:

- What is your destination and end goal for the strategic plan?
- Do you want your staff more aligned and connected or restructure how they interact?
- Has your budget changed and now you need to dial in what priorities as a department you need to focus on?
- What direction are you headed in?
- Has there been a change in leadership that may lead to a reduction or restructure in staff?
- Do you need to adjust your communication strategies to build rapport with new leadership?
- Who do you want to bring along with you?
- Are there some colleagues in other departments you can build alliances with to strengthen your cause?
- What will they need for the trip ahead?
- Will your team need equipment, education for new technology or software being rolled out?
- What questions, resistance, problems, and challenges do you foresee from your team before you begin?
- Do you need to carve out some time and space to allow for feedback or pushback as you walk through this process?

There isn't a right or wrong way to go about this as you plan strategically. The critical thing is to plan.

Fresh Eyes

When it comes to charting your course, sometimes you need a fresh pair of eyes. As leaders, we tend to look at everything through the same old lens. What has worked before works great, until it stops working. In 2010 I was working with Texas Football under Coach Mack Brown and our season wasn't going as planned. We had come off a very successful year losing to Alabama in the National Championship 37-21. We were one game shy of being champions. That year we reloaded our team with talent and it seemed very promising. We planned to pick right back where we left off. That season we ended going 5-7 and failed to reach a bowl game, something Texas Football had not done since the pre-Mack Brown era. Fans and donors were upset. The 2010 season was tough, but Coach Brown knew what he had to do. He brought in a close colleague from outside of our organization to evaluate what was going on. His job was simple. He spent an entire week with us and observed. He attended meetings, came to practice, and interacted with players and staff. His goal wasn't to disrupt anything but to be a fly on the wall.

Sometimes as leaders we are too close to the fire. When pressures and problems arise it helps to bring in a fresh pair of eyes. Your view of your own problems can tend to be subjective. Your judgment can become clouded and you become frustrated and overwhelmed, and stressed out. You are too close to the problem because you are right in the middle of it. When you bring someone in from the outside, they tend to be more objective. They have an ability to view things with a fresh perspective. They don't carry the same emotional investment and they aren't in the trenches day to day. One of my favorite authors on leadership, Andy Stanley, talks about the importance of this principle when he states, "The longer you've served where you are and the longer you've done what you are currently doing, the more difficult it will be for you to see your environments with the objectivity needed to make the changes that need to be made. Time in erodes awareness of."[12] In essence, the longer you lead in your current role the harder it is to clearly see what is going on and what needs to change. Bring fresh eyes in.

Let's look at five principles to guide you before bringing fresh eyes in:

1. **Choose Carefully** – Don't pick your buddy and bring them in to tell you what you want to hear. Doing so has the potential to make matters worse. Do your homework and bring in someone who has credibility and success in your field. Find someone who will be honest with you, won't sugar coat what they see, and will keep your organization's best interest in mind.

2. **Paint a Broad Picture** – When you bring in fresh eyes, have them look at the entire picture. They don't necessarily need to get into the weeds, but they do need to observe and see the main areas that impact your success or failure. Depending on how you do this, it might entail setting up some meetings with the heads of each department. It may include time to watch and observe your staff while they are working together or serving customers. It could also involve sending out a survey before they arrive to gather some general information about your company, team, or staff. You would be amazed at how easily you can shift course so slightly that you don't even notice it.

3. **Manage the Tension** – No matter how you slice it, any time you bring someone from outside your organization or team into the mix, it will cause tension. People will be on high alert

and may put up walls or be very guarded. Bringing in fresh eyes can be viewed as a threat, especially if jobs are on the line or problem areas are being evaluated. No matter what the situation, work to manage and diffuse the tension. The best way to do this is to minimize disruption as much as possible. If you sound the alarm and rally the troops everyone will be tense, and it will be a distraction. The more you can make it just like a normal day the better results and take aways you will have. If appropriate and possible, let your people know who is coming in and why. It still may not sit well with them but if you can calm their fears and reassure them of the purpose they won't be caught off guard. At the end of the day, you are trying to right the ship and come up with some solutions for the current problems you are dealing with.

4. **After Action Review** – Once the person you have brought in as a consultant has finished observing, have them compile their thoughts, notes, and observations into one document. Schedule a time to sit down with them individually as well as with your leadership team to review the observations. Provide everyone an opportunity to review the information, make notes, ask questions, and seek deeper explanations of what is going on. Open the group up to possible solutions not yet considered. The biggest goal for the after-action review is to walk away with clarity of what the pressing problems are as well as to identify what solutions you want to see implemented moving forward. Seek for execution and accountability once the dust has settled. Practically speaking, set some dates to follow up and get feedback on what has changed. Has anything

improved? What is working? Has it gotten worse? The more specific feedback you can get the better.

5. **Make the Tough Call** – Being the leader means the buck stops with you. The year Texas football went 5-7, Coach Brown had to make some very difficult changes on staff. It was hard and uncomfortable. Tension was high, and we were all on high alert, fearful of losing our jobs. It wasn't easy but it was necessary. When you bring in fresh eyes, be prepared to face the music. More than likely if things aren't going well, there is a reason. As a leader you will need to address this head on, have some uncomfortable conversations, and make some difficult changes. This is the essence of leadership. When the ship goes off course, the captain must do whatever it takes to make the necessary changes to right the ship.

Reflect for a moment and ask yourself: what course are you on? Are you heading in the right direction? Do you need a course correction? Is your vision outdated and needs a refresh? Are you planning out the main goals and objectives you want to accomplish or are you winging it? Is it time to bring some fresh eyes in and get timely feedback and advice on why you have been struggling lately? Do you need to create a greater sense of urgency by setting some deadlines on changes you want to see implemented? No matter what the situation or scenario, charting your course is a critical part of leadership. Leaders are taking their people on a journey. They are going somewhere. Make sure you are on a mission and that the course you set is the one you want to be one.

CHAPTER 3
Dirty Jobs

"I don't pay to have my dirty work done for me, I do it myself."

Ted Nugent

Getting Your Hands Dirty on Paperwork

Growing up in the country, you might find yourself doing some of the hardest, dirtiest jobs imaginable. I grew up in Gallatin, a small town in Tennessee, not too far from Kentucky. My family built a home in a rural area where we owned and cared for six wild horses on five acres of land. Most of the time, I enjoyed the work of caring for horses. Keep them contained, feed them, give them their shots, trim their hooves, and spend time with them regularly. It was work, but rewarding and enjoyable. One winter, we needed to prepare the area of the barn where the horses sheltered on freezing nights. It was a small barn that was filled with hay to keep them warm throughout the night. The problem was that the stall was also packed with manure and if we didn't clean it out, it was highly likely that they would develop health issues or even catch a disease. My dad informed me that I had the pleasure of shoveling months' worth of stomped and trampled horse poop and wheeling it into the open pasture as fertilizer. The smell was horrid, the labor was strenuous, and I felt like I would never get the odor out of my clothes and hair. I do not remember how long it took, but I remember hating doing it. In the end, the horses had a clean stall and made it through the winter healthy and thriving and I learned a valuable lesson of putting in the work doing the necessary things, no matter how hard they were to get done.

If your goal is to lead one day, you will have to get your hands dirty. Though not as physically strenuous as cleaning out a horse barn, some people equally despise doing paperwork. In the early years of my career, I detested paperwork so much that I would do anything to avoid it. If my supervisors were looking for volunteers to help push some papers, I would get real quiet or make a hasty exit. Why was I so opposed to paperwork? Simply put, I didn't know what I was doing and for me, paperwork was intimidating. Anything requiring physical work or skill always came easily to me and I was happy to put the work in, but the organizational and clerical skill required to properly complete paperwork terrified me.

As a leader, you will grow familiar with business processes and most of these processes have associated paperwork. Travel requests, budget creation, effective communication, drafting project proposals, paying bills, placing purchase orders, laying out capital projects, renewing contracts, and keeping track of expenses are just a few paperwork jobs you may run into. An effective leader needs to manage two things effectively:

1. **People work** – managing and overseeing others.

2.	**Paperwork** – managing protocols and procedures.

While people are paramount for any job you will ever do, don't think for a second paperwork isn't important. Paperwork can be a dirty job that no one looks forward to doing, but it must be done. Keeping current records, forms and documents on every single thing you do as a leader is not only necessary, but if done diligently will help you become a better leader. There is a relational side to leading, but let's not forget that there is a business side that, if neglected, will hinder you from doing your job effectively.

As a younger coach, I thought very differently than I do today. I failed to see the importance of paperwork. I considered myself a coach, not an administrator. One day, after leading our strength camps I realized the importance of properly handled processes. That one summer of directing our camps forced me to do so much paperwork that I finally got over the fear of doing it. The more detailed, efficient, and accurate the business side of coaching was, the better I could coach. The two worked hand in hand. That summer gave me the confidence boost I needed to grow as a professional and see that I was fully capable of leading and managing others as well as the department. What I once thought of as a dirty job became the very vehicle that set me on a path to director years down the road. Let's look at five reasons for you to consider to start doing more paperwork:

1.	**Learning Your Job Inside and Out** – If you really want to be the best at what you do, you need to know, at minimum, a base level of every aspect of your job and how it all works together as a unit. I'm not saying you need to get your MBA, but there are great benefits to knowing what processes are involved behind the scenes. When I was put in charge of making sure our equipment was regularly maintained, I had to start dealing with phone calls, purchase orders, mis-priced parts, workers who didn't follow through, machines that didn't work right after being repaired, and companies who tried to overcharge us. I gained a new appreciation of companies that ran a tight ship, but also a new respect for our administrators that have to deal with problems. Oftentimes, what you see and what actually happens behind the scenes are two different things. What might seem easy, is actually very hard work and hours have been invested so it can operate smoothly and safely. Being involved and learning the ins and outs of your job will make you more appreciative and an all around better leader.

2. **Paying Attention to Details** – The best leaders pay attention to the little things. Detail orientation is one mark that will not only set you apart, but make you stand out. Though it's not always fun, staying consistent with completing paperwork and paying attention to details will be a habit that will serve you well your entire career. The longer you lead, the more often you will experience times where someone needs a document, receipt, or clarification on something you have done in the past. When you do the little things with excellence, you will look like a rock star! You will become a person everyone knows they can count on and can trust to do things right.

3. **Keep From Wasting Time** – One of the biggest ways people waste time is looking for things they can't find. When you start handling paperwork, it will force you to get more organized.

The more organized you are, the more efficient and productive you will become. Developing an effective system of how you think, process, handle and file paperwork will take you to the next level as a leader. I have worked with coaches over the years who were not organized and they were almost always negligent on getting things done in a timely fashion. Their inability to prioritize and effectively complete tasks caused someone else to have to take their time to get the job completed. Time was wasted looking for things they could not find simply because they did not manage it well.

4. **Increase Your Influence** – If you are a person who hates paperwork, hear me out for a second. Your influence will grow immensely over time and you will be viewed as a leader by others in your organization. By becoming more administrative, you will start interacting more with people in the business office you never would meet if you didn't. By working with others outside your area, you will begin to build new relationships with them. If you treat others well and are easy to work with, your reputation will grow and your name will gain recognition. This is accomplished one conversation, interaction, and document at a time. Some of your transactions might be over email or phone but do not underestimate how much influence you can build over time simply through normal everyday business interactions. Though it may seem small and insignificant, there will come a time you will either need something done, or need someone in a higher position to help you push a decision through and you will get it done all because you have built solid relationships over time.

5. **CYA (Cover Your Ass)** – Every business involves risk. When risk is involved, there is always the potential of some threat looming. Learning how to do paperwork will help protect you. Whether it's handling employee conflict, dealing with fiscal discrepancies, or just plain old accidents that happen in normal everyday life, you will want to cover your rear end and look out for yourself. If you do not do this, you are putting yourself in an exposed and vulnerable position that can damage your reputation and possibly even end your career. At the end of the day, you must take full responsibility for how you handle your business. You will be held accountable for any missteps that occur. Paperwork or "leaving a paper trail" can cover you, to a degree, because it is physical proof you have been transparent and up front in all transactions. It shows you have a system of checks and balances to hold you accountable. If you spend money on an item and the account ledger comes back you are short a certain amount, you can go back and show where the inaccuracy is. If you have a heated conversation with an employee and they end up filing a complaint against you because you upset them for holding them accountable over the weeks or months of not doing quality work, you will be covered when you show a detailed record of conversations and actions you have taken. If not, it can become your word against theirs. Remember this, the harder you work, the higher you will climb. The higher you climb, the greater the stakes involved. With higher stakes, come greater consequences for not doing things right. Doing paperwork, though a dirty job, will help you do your job right and cover you when something goes wrong.

Consider where you are in your career currently. No matter where you are, paperwork will most likely be an unavoidable part of your job. Just like when I was young and had to help my dad clean out the horse barn after it had been neglected, there comes a time when you have to handle jobs you don't want to do. You can't just keep avoiding it. Get your hands dirty doing paperwork. Develop this skill set and you will be better prepared for career opportunities that come your way. It will give those interviewing you the confidence that you are a good manager and steward of the resources they will be entrusting you with.

Run to the Roar

Years ago at a conference, I learned a hard lesson about dealing with dirty jobs. I had just become a director and initially everything seemed to be going great, that was until I began having some staff issues. I will spare you the details, but ultimately a staff member was unwilling to comply and simply not doing what I had asked them to do. They kept ignoring my instructions and doing what they wanted to do. Naively, I hoped for the best and waited for the issue to resolve itself but not only did it not go away, it got much worse. The little things turned into bigger things and started wearing negatively on the rest of the staff. Now, not only was I dealing with one problematic staff member, I was also dealing with other staff members who were impacted and complaining about it. Out of fear of confrontation, I continued to avoid the situation thinking being nice and staying positive would solve it.

During this conference, I first heard the words "Run to the Roar"[13]. The speaker shared an old African teaching about fear. When young lions are hungry and searching for food, they send the oldest, weakest member of the pride to lie in the grass and wait for the herds of gazelle to pass by. The old lion has lost most of his teeth and isn't strong enough to chase and capture prey, however, his roar is very loud and intimidating and can strike fear into the hearts of its next meal. When the herd of gazelle comes near the hunting pack of young lions, the old lion lets loose a loud roar causing the gazelle to flee away from the roar. The loud roar startles the gazelle causing them to run towards the hungry pack of young lions, and consequently straight to their deaths. The meaning of the parable is simple. Don't run from fear, run to it. If we run from problems because we are afraid, like the gazelles running from the roar, it can actually cause us harm.

As a leader you will experience fear. It can be political pressure, department restructures, making mistakes, not making your quarterly numbers, having a staff member going maverick on you, or your personal life threatening your job. No matter the situation, whether it is small or big, run to the roar. Hearing the parable that day was life changing for me as a leader. My approach with one of our staff was not working. I was running from the roar. I was fearful of confrontation and wasn't addressing behaviors because I didn't want to offend them. Upon returning to work from that conference, I had a new perspective. I saw how fear was driving me to lead in a way I knew wasn't working. I made the decision to run to the roar and address the employee and the issues head on. No more avoidance and dancing around the problem, no more sugar coating the situation. It was time for me to run to the roar. Let's look at five truths about facing your fears:

1. **The Problem Isn't as Big as You Think** – Fear does a funny thing in your head. It taunts you and tells you that your fear is much worse than it really is, causing you to shrink back and not deal. As long as you listen to the voice of fear you keep quiet and say nothing. "Don't rock the boat," fear warns you, "If you confront it, it will backfire and you will be defeated." Fear thrives in the dark and comes off seeming much bigger than it really is. Once you gain the courage to face your fear, you'll find it usually isn't as big and as bad as you thought.

2. **Facing Fear Will Strengthen Your Courage** – Every leader needs to be courageous at some point. You will need to take a stand. You cannot keep running from problems. Facing your fear gives you courage. Like a muscle, the more you use it, the stronger it becomes. Running from the roar is refusing to use the strength you have. Like a muscle, it atrophies. The more you run from your fears the weaker you will become as a leader. Take courage and don't back down. Stand your ground.

3. **Fear Can Cause Strong Emotions** – When you face your fears, it can be very difficult. You will tremble in your boots at times, and that is ok. Feel the fear and do it anyway. Don't let an emotional surge of fear paralyze you from doing what you know needs to be done. When the gazelle hears the loud roar, if they actually ran to the roar they would be safe because the old lion is weak and toothless. In a similar fashion, fear intimidates you and keeps you away. As long as you keep running and avoiding problems, fear will continue to defeat you.

4. **Courage Is Contagious** – Courage has the ability to change the environment and embolden others around you. In the same

way fear paralyzes, courage moves others to take action. Leadership is about setting an example. People don't do what you say, they do what they see. Facing your fears in small matters can rub off on others and have a profound effect and change people's lives drastically.

5. **Courage Can Save Your Life** – If they ran to the roar, the gazelles would have found safety. As leaders we have to run to the roar, because that is where real safety/solutions are found. It won't always feel comfortable, but if you continue to avoid problems, pressures, and dealing with difficult staff, it will eventually catch up to you. Turn and face whatever it is that you are avoiding. Confront it. Schedule the meeting. Have the conversation. Make the change. Face the difficulty. In doing so, you will find courage to press on and deal with the issue at hand.

I learned something from my experience of avoiding a troublesome staff member. Not only should you run to the roar, don't wait to do it. Don't delay. The sooner you move towards whatever is holding you back, the better chance you have at fixing it. The situation ended up working out for everyone, but I should have acted more quickly. Not making a decision is making a decision. Stalling, procrastinating, putting off dirty jobs, and avoiding crucial conversations with staff never makes anything better. Take courage, face your fears, and run to the roar.

Pull the Tooth

The morning after the last game of our 1991 regular season, I was awakened early by an intense burning pain in my jaw. I was trying to sleep in after a night of celebrating our victory over the Yellow Jackets of Georgia Tech who we had defeated in a 4th quarter barn-burner 18-15! The pain was so bad that I couldn't bite down or even close my jaw. The tissue around my back teeth was swollen and my face was puffy. I had ignorantly spent the week shrugging off the nagging pain. That night, I tried to go back to sleep, but the pain pounded in my jaw like my heart had moved into that joint. I finally gave up on sleep, naively hoping that as my day went on, the pain would recede. It did not. My bite was completely restricted, and I couldn't eat. I went to see our team doctor when I got back to Athens and he announced that my wisdom teeth were trying to come in and there wasn't room in my mouth for them. One of the teeth was impacted, infected, and swollen. He recommended I see the dentist immediately, but it was the week of Thanksgiving and I could not schedule an appointment with a dentist until after the holiday. For three days I endured severe pain and swelling. The dentist confirmed what our team doctor had diagnosed and gave me two options. Pull two wisdom teeth on one side or pull all four at once and never deal with the problem again. After the intense pain I endured since neglecting the issue, the decision was simple: pull all four wisdom teeth! There was no way I wanted to go through this experience ever again. I knew my decision would be painful and recovery would be much longer but I didn't care. The pain of pulling the teeth would be well worth the price so I wouldn't go through this again.

As we continue the topic of dirty, not-so-fun jobs, this story serves as an analogy. When leading, you will inevitably at some point deal with a staff member who causes pain to you and your staff. Often the pain doesn't seem harmful at first, just a nagging issue that you can endure. They may be difficult to talk to at times, not easy to work with for other departments, poor listeners, or perhaps it's something even more subtle like being chronically late for work or key appointments. No matter the shape or form, unresolved problems will add up over time and just like my tooth causing pain discomfort, the unresolved issues can permeate your department.

As a leader, I know this: there will be jobs and tasks no one likes doing, but if you do not do them, it will cost you. The part of leadership no one ever talks about is the messy stuff. In this instance, I am talking about firing someone. That person, no matter how many chances you give them or how patient you are with them, it simply is not working out. It is time to let them go. At first, you may speak with them to correct the issues at hand and you may even see improvement and effort on their part. You think to yourself, "I handled that well and now they will not do it again". The issue persists, and something else happens. As a good leader, you address the issue again. You think again, "Now we are good! Problem solved". Unfortunately however, if repeatedly addressing the issue isn't solving the problem, I can wager to say, it's not going away. Like my tooth throbbing that morning in Atlanta, there is only one solution that will fix it. Pull the tooth! At the end of the day if we are really going to lead well, we have got to get better at making tough decisions. Let's look at five key practices to walk through to help you with the process of firing someone:

I. **Confront, Correct, and Counsel** – Before you ever even think about getting rid of someone, you have got to make sure you have done everything in your power to help them be successful. This means you need to have difficult conversations with them about where they have fallen short in the job or your expectations. Keep in mind whenever you do this you have to be specific. Using vague generalities like "you seem" or "bad attitude" will not help you nor them. It will only make it more frustrating. Be very specific about an instance or instances of what they did and how it negatively impacted those involved. Once they are clear on what went wrong and are aware of it, provide them with some counsel on how they can improve next time.

2. **Document** – When working with a staff member to make adjustments/improvements and you don't see any effort or improvement, you will need to be diligent about documenting each of the instances where you met to address the concern. I typically like to give new employees extra grace when coming on staff since it's pretty much impossible to not have some issues until they get acclimated and adjusted to the company culture and policies. However, when you continue to deal with the same issues and there is no visible improvement, it is imperative to have documentation stating when and how the concerns were addressed. A log detailing what days you met, what the issues were and how it was addressed, as well as any action you took to help correct the problem and how the meeting went. In my opinion, as a leader your people deserve some time and opportunity to get it right, but you have to cover your bases with detailed steps of how you have worked with them to remedy the issues at hand.

3. **Take It to the Next Level** – If the problem continues and there is no improvement, you have reached a critical stage

of firing someone. I recommend you have conversations and communicate with your HR department in detail about the issues. Oftentimes, this step can be a reality check for you to ensure that you are handling the situation correctly within your company's policies. As a leader, it is your responsibility to do your homework and find out. On top of that, your HR department may have access to professional services to help prevent someone from being fired like mentoring or one-on-one coaching.

4. **Make the Decision** – There will come a day when you have to make the decision that it's just not working. Continuing to try and fit a round peg in a square hole only frustrates the employee causing the problems, as well as those they are working with. Stay within the policies and guidelines of HR, but make the decision and move forward.

5. **Take the High Road** – Firing someone is very heart wrenching. It's hard for you but it's even harder for the person getting fired. Do your best to remove the emotion. For the person being terminated, it can be embarrassing, hurtful, and cause intense anxiety, shame or fear. Have compassion on how you deliver the news. You can do it in a way that leaves a door open so you can be a part of the process to help them pick up the pieces and move forward. Taking the high road is mentally preparing yourself to be ready for how the person getting fired may respond. They may blow up, cry, yell, clam up, curse, or even seem bewildered or confused. Be ready to show compassion, empathy and support no matter how they react. What you don't want to do is put more salt in the wound and cause

more pain by responding in a way that seems harsh or cold. You have no control over how they react or respond, but you do over yours. If they act in a way that is unprofessional or do something they may later regret, they can come back and apologize and fix it if they want. On the other hand, if you act in a way that is harmful, you run the risk of ruining or destroying the relationship. From my experience, taking the high road is treating them better than they deserve in that moment which has the power to retain your relationship with them down the road for any future involvements. In the crazy world of coaching and business you never know when you may end up having to work alongside them again in years to come. How you treat someone during difficult decisions says a lot about you as a leader.

The Dirtiest Job on the Planet

What is the dirtiest job you have ever had to complete? I remember mine vividly. When we built our home, it was outside the city limits and situated too far from the main road to have access to sewage lines, so we had to install a septic system to our house. Living in a large house in the country with eight occupants means high water usage and a lot of strain on the plumbing. Everything was going great the first few years we lived there. Every year my dad would call a company to empty out the septic tank until one year, when money was short and my dad couldn't afford to pay the company to empty the tank. Safe to say, that was a regrettable circumstance. As I'm sure you can deduce, the lines started backing up in our house. Water backed up when we washed clothes, did the dishes, or showered. Eventually the drainage water would go back down, but it was a warning the tank was full and action needed to be taken ASAP!

Since we didn't have the funds to call someone, my dad decided we would have to manage this situation ourselves. First, we had to locate the cap to the tank which was buried somewhere in the backyard. After digging up several patches of grass, we eventually found the cap and removed it. To put it nicely, it was disgusting. My dad brought out the pump and we lowered it into the tank. It took several miserable stinky hours, but we eventually got the job done and were able to resume normal life in our house. It was the most revolting job I have ever done or hope to ever do again.

Firing someone is a dirty job no matter how you look at it. It hurts, it's hard, it stresses you out, you lose sleep over it, you try to avoid it but at the end of the day, you must squeeze the trigger and decide. It is the dirtiest job in the world as a leader. Anytime you let someone go you impact their livelihood. Their security will be threatened and many times emotions take control. It is paramount that you as a leader maintain a calm demeanor and a high level of professionalism when you have to terminate an employee. Let's look at five reasons you cannot avoid this responsibility if you want to continue to be successful and progress in your career in the years ahead:

1. **People Are Messy** – The majority of problems a leader encounters are people problems. The answer to most of those problems will also be people. Leadership is dealing with and managing people. People's problems are not always easy, simple, and microwavable. Managing people will take time because their issues can be complex. As a leader, you will

be required to step into situations and take action. Firing people will be a decision you have to make. It will be messy. Difficult, uncomfortable, and confrontational conversations must be had.

2. **The Situation Will Get Worse before It Gets Better** – One reason leaders avoid firing someone is the situation doesn't typically improve immediately. The main issue was addressed, but the problem is still there to be cleaned up. One of the biggest mistakes I have made was putting off the inevitable. I wanted to be patient, working with the staff member, overlooking mishaps, giving them more chances, all to avoid letting them go. But in my indecision, staff morale dropped, problems continued and eventually the pressure grew to a level I could no longer ignore. By not doing what I needed to do, I was hurting my staff, other departments, and losing credibility as a leader. I had to make the hard decision.

3. **It Keeps Your Department from Staff Unity and Getting to the Next Level** – If you keep avoiding the inevitable, you are holding your staff and department back. It's like there is a weight or barrier holding everyone down. Once the barrier is removed or remedied, everyone feels it immediately. The log jam is cleared and suddenly, things can move forward. That is how problems work, take away the issue and consequently morale is strengthened and all the energy you had been putting towards the person not working out, can be put towards something more positive.

4. **You Help the Person Getting Fired Move Forward** – As harsh as it may sound, letting an employee go can be instrumental in

helping them to move forward. Until you let them go, they are often just stuck. To be fired from a job is hurtful, but whether we like it or not, sometimes the most painful seasons of our lives teach us lessons we could not learn otherwise.

5. **You Care about Them as a Leader and Boss** – Anytime you let someone go, there should be a process you follow. If you call yourself a leader and you hire someone, it is imperative you show them you care by giving them feedback, coaching, and providing input as you go.

As we conclude this chapter on a very touchy and difficult topic, remember this: the biggest problems we will have to deal with at work are people. Oftentimes the best solution to our problems at work will be people! Either way you slice it, you have got to get really good at managing and dealing with people. Enjoy the fun and exciting times of hiring great staff but also recognize the messy and stressful times of letting someone go. Both are critically necessary if you want to be a great leader! Don't forget that you are making a decision to make you and your department better. I refer back to when I woke up in the dentist chair the day they removed all four of my wisdom teeth. I felt wonky, weird and a little off but one thing for sure, I was pain free and now I could focus on healing and getting better. Pulling the tooth is necessary. It hurts, but if done right it opens opportunities for healing and growth in the department.

CHAPTER 4

Engagement and Empowerment

> "Empowerment is what managers do to people,
> engagement is what managers do with people."
>
> Henry Minztberg

Walk Slowly Through the Halls

The day I took over running our summer camps I was somewhat terrified. The woman who was the point person for all paperwork and financials was small, tough, direct, and at times intimidating. She didn't play any games. I never had to deal with her up to this point, but I knew if I got off on the wrong foot with her, it wouldn't go well for me. At first, it was all business – I did exactly what she said. I would come in, give her everything she needed and leave. No small talk, no connection, and no interaction. I knew if we were going to work well together I needed to try something to break through with her. One day I happened to be walking past her office and decided to casually poke my head in and say hello. I had no agenda, but wanted to swing by and be friendly. As I stopped by,

I can't remember if she even looked up and acknowledged me but I do recall the next time I had to go see her for business, she seemed more open and friendly. There was something a little different in a positive way with our interaction.

For the next several months, I would stop by and say hello and occasionally ask how she was doing. Before long, we ended up sitting and visiting one day after I had dropped off some paperwork and she began to share how her family was doing. It wasn't a long conversation but it really made a difference in our interactions. She was more human to me now. She wasn't just the stern, unapproachable business woman who scared me to death. I admired and respected her because of the love for her family. I found out she worked so hard because she was the primary breadwinner of her family. If she didn't make a living her family would suffer. Over the next few years we continued to work together and became close colleagues. She became the main person who helped me navigate a large purchase request for new equipment that was initially denied. She operated with such integrity and developed great relationships with the "higher ups", and she was able to help me get the request approved so we could move forward. She remains someone I admire and respect to this day.

This story illustrates a principle about leadership: walk slowly through the halls. Take time to visit with people and get to know them. We live in such a fast and superficial world today. Nobody seems to have time for anything or anyone anymore. When you walk slowly through the halls, you send a message to others that they matter. You value them as humans. As a leader, your ability to convey care and value to your colleagues will be the most critical element. A survey of 400 employed Americans reveals that 2 in 3 (67%) say they don't always feel appreciated for their contributions at work. In addition, nearly half (42%) of respondents feel their company lacks a strong culture of appreciation.[14] Maya Angelou says "People will forget what you said, people will forget what you did but people will never forget how you made them feel."[15] When you walk slowly through the halls, people will know you value and appreciate them. It may be the golden rule of leadership. You must show people you care about them before you can lead them. People will follow a boss because they have to but if you want to have influence as a leader, start slowing down and spend some time getting to know them. Communicating value and appreciation takes time, investment, and energy but it is worth every moment. Let's take a look at five reasons why you should get out of the office and walk slowly through the halls:

1. **Job Satisfaction** – The more intentional relationships you build at work, the happier you will be, and you will actually look forward to going to work. When you walk slowly through the halls you will meet people you might never run into otherwise. Over time, those relationships will pay off when you end up working with them on a project, or needing their help with an issue. I cannot tell you how many times asking for help from another department was easier because we had an existing relationship.

2. **Personal Brand** – What do others say about you when you are not around? Do they see you as unapproachable, unfriendly, stuck up, or offish? Are there some people who don't even know who you are or is there someone you have never met before? Remember every person you work with directly or indirectly has an opinion of you. Right or wrong, they have one. Walking

slowly through the halls has the ability to change someone's perception of you. A short, positive interaction forms an impression in a person's mind. The experience forms a memory in their brain. The more you interact with them in a positive way, the story they tell others about you becomes your personal brand. If you want to lead one day your personal brand matters. It will be a big influence on who wants to work with you and who doesn't.

3. **Selflessness** – The best leaders are focused on others. They love working with others for a common purpose and mission. As you learn to lead, doing your job will be a challenge at times. If not careful, you can get lost along the way. Without realizing it, you can become so mission focused you forget it takes people to accomplish the goal. Walking slowly through the halls keeps you grounded by forming a habit of staying human and not getting wrapped up in yourself. If you are not careful the people you work with can become a means to an end. If you see others for what they can do for you rather than what they mean to you, you can become self-centered. Walking slowly through the halls keeps you in touch with the real world and helps you remember what is most important: the value of your people.

4. **Future Problems** – If you want to lead, you will encounter problems. Some will be small and some will seem insurmountable but you will not be able to avoid entanglements. When you get out of your office and take time to get to know people, especially in other areas or departments, they will become an advocate for you. They may end up being someone you can

go to or lean on when you run into roadblocks. If you remain on an island, you will experience some lonely battles. Life is a team sport and especially if you want to lead effectively. As John Maxwell says "Leaders touch a heart before they ask for a hand."[16]

5. **Effective Management** – The best leaders keep a pulse on how their staff is doing. How's the morale in the office? Who is struggling or going through a rough personal season? When you walk slowly through the halls, check in on your people. Additionally, when you have to share some negative news to the staff or key personnel, the timing and delivery of that message will change if you know what's going on in the office. Leading others isn't about being a dictator and telling others what to do all the time. That may work at first, but over time your influence will wane. Carefully navigating challenging situations with compassion goes a long way. It can be the difference between someone staying with you or searching for another job.

Do you walk the halls? Are you a person who bunkers down in the office all the time and doesn't interact with others? Do you come in, do your job, and leave for the day with minimal interaction? I want to encourage you to get out of the office more. Get out of the ivory tower. Don't send an email for a request, go to the person's office and speak to them. If you are running an errand to an area or department you have never been, stop and introduce yourself and visit briefly. Be respectful of people's time and always be cognizant of if they are in the middle of something. Until you get to know them better, keep the interactions high and tight. Over time, you will learn to read others and if it's a good time to visit with them. By walking slowly through the halls, you may not always get everything done but you will accomplish the most important checklist as a leader: letting people know you value them.

The Power of Appreciation

It was National Boss's day and I had secretly called a meeting for all our staff in the coach's lounge. I wanted to take some time and surprise our boss with a cake and card of appreciation. When he came downstairs, he was completely caught off guard. He cautiously followed me into the room where everyone was gathered, staring at him with possum grins on their faces. He slowly walked and joined the circle and looked worried. "Relax coach," I said, "this is a positive meeting. Today is National Boss's Day and we wanted to surprise you!" His reaction was priceless. "Oh my God," he exclaimed. "You guys had me so worried!" We all had a good laugh at his reaction..

The event, though small and insignificant, opened my eyes. We tend to meet only when there is a problem, or singling people out when a mistake has been made. We are not great at recognizing people and showing them appreciation. We are drawn to those who honor us. Think about someone who has been your biggest cheerleader, a person who has believed in you when others didn't. Who are those who look up to you and speak well about you, especially in front of others? You are drawn to them like a magnet in your heart. We naturally gravitate to friends, family, or colleagues who show appreciation and honor us in even the smallest of ways. Here's the secret sauce though: if you want to lead people well, you must sincerely show them how much you appreciate them. If you make time to correct them when things go wrong, then take time to thank them and appreciate them when something goes right. Demonstrating appreciation need not be a spectacle but make it a habit. A study of 200,000 managers and employees in Fast Company magazine found that 79% of people who quit their jobs cite lack of appreciation as a major reason for leaving.[17] They are working hard for a boss or a company but no one is taking notice and rewarding their effort. If you are not appreciated and valued for what you do, dissatisfaction will fester. Everyone likes to be rewarded for their hard work. Some like it publicly and some like it privately but either way, it's a fundamental need. Showing appreciation goes a long way with people. Let's look at five practical ways to help create a workplace where others are appreciated:

1. **Pay Attention** – Watch your people. What time do they come in everyday? How many hours are they working each week? How much time did they spend on a project? How often do they deliver on time? Do they make your job easier? Are they always in a positive mood? Stop and pay attention and you will find so many ways people work hard with excellence. Lou Tice wrote a book called *Coaching for Personal Results*[18], and tells the story of a man who managed a boy's orphan house. Despite all his effort, this man could not get the boys to improve their behavior. After weeks and weeks of failed attempts to get the orphaned boys to comply, he brought in a counselor to observe and help. For one week the counselor stayed in the house and watched, took notes, and observed how the boys interacted with the house manager. Sharing what he saw, the counselor pointed out that the house manager was great at catching

and correcting the boys anytime they did something wrong, but not once did he ever reward one of the boys for doing something right. From that day forward, the house manager changed his approach and the results were incredible. Within weeks, the boys started showing signs of positive behavior and compliance. What gets rewarded in life gets repeated!

2. **Surprise, Surprise, Surprise** – One of the best ways to really show appreciation is to surprise them. This may take some planning but the payoff is worth it. In Chip and Dan Heath's life changing book, *The Power of Moments*[19] they illustrate how there are times in our lives where we can create special moments that galvanize in our memories and emotions and change how we think, act, and feel about a person or place. What might have a history of negative experiences can be completely changed just by creating small moments from good experiences. One example they used was how pediatric staff decorated their MRI with jungle decor for children who were terrified of the big, loud machine. By creating a jungle in and around the machine, they transformed terror into adventure. The same can happen when we plan small, insignificant moments at work and turn them into acts of appreciation.

3. **Speak Their Appreciation Language** – Do some homework on how your people receive appreciation. What one person loves another may hate. What motivates him, may demotivate her. When it comes to appreciation, one size does not fit all. Some people like to get off work a little early. Some like flexible work hours. Some like awards and bonuses. Some like big plaques with their names on it. Others may be mortified if you called

their name out in front of a large audience. Some people really know you appreciate them when you ask how their family or kids are doing. Others want more privacy. Whatever it is, find out how each individual receives appreciation, and demonstrate their value to them.

4. **Extra Sauce** – If someone works really hard for you and they do a great job, go out of your way to bring recognition to it. Point it out. You can do this in a staff meeting, or if they don't like being singled out, you can do it privately in person. Whatever way you choose, don't let it slip by and overlook it. If someone runs an errand for you that is out of their way as part of the job, buy them a coffee or breakfast. Let them come in later the next day as a thank you. Don't demand or expect loyalty, earn it. Even the smallest acts of appreciation over time has the power to transform how people do their jobs on a daily basis.

5. **Small Perks** – Little things make big differences. When you give your staff small perks and privileges they don't normally get, it sends a message that they matter to you. It sends a message that you care. I remember early in my career our staff was fortunate enough to receive a small stipend from our head coach for Nike shoes and gear to order. We had never received a perk like this before. It blew us away. Our head coach fought to get it because he felt we deserved it for all our hard work. Looking back now it wasn't much money at the time, but the impact it had on our department was huge. It made us feel appreciated and valued. It motivated us to go the extra mile and want to work harder for our head coach. When you feel appreciated you don't mind bending over backwards for someone. Being

a leader who shows appreciation will help your staff reach for new heights and build a healthy and positive work culture, as well as employee loyalty. One of the main reasons I surprised my boss on national boss day was because I wanted to change the environment and culture. I had been promoted to a position of manager and I wanted to send a message to my boss and my coworkers that what they do matters! As leaders we cannot always change everything we want but you can make sure the changes you do make have a big impact. Showing appreciation can and will do that if you will just try.

Empowering Others

Leaders need to learn to let go. For many, letting go can be a very difficult and challenging thing to do. If you love to micromanage you may be successful at what you do, but you will never allow those you are leading to become all they could be. Leadership isn't just about doing great things, it's also about developing great people. You need both to be a great leader. I would rather be great at developing those around me over being seen as successful because of what I can do by myself. The leaders I have met, studied, and learned from over the years were always bigger than themselves. Their leadership helped those around them grow and get better. These were leaders who empowered others.

Empowerment is not just giving responsibility. Anyone can delegate tasks and tell people what to do but it takes a leader to empower others. Empowerment begins with showing support and backing those you are leading. You give them responsibility, but you also give them the authority to do their jobs. To be effective you must have both. When you give someone authority you are giving them autonomy. You don't micromanage them by looking over their shoulder every single moment and always have an opinion about what they are doing. You offer input and counsel depending on the situation, but you also let them make decisions and lead.

Is it dangerous to give others authority? You bet it is. You run the risk of not having something done the way you would do it. The best leaders are secure in releasing some of their power. Leaders empower those around them to learn, lead, and leverage the skills, talents, and unique abilities they possess. Let's briefly discuss five reasons why empowerment is so effective when done correctly:

1. **Engagement** – If you want better engagement from your staff, learn to empower them. Give them your support, backing, and confidence. When I was given the task of designing a new training facility for our Olympic sports at The University of Texas, I had to research different equipment companies and create a layout that would service the teams and space we were given. As I began the process, I enlisted one of our staff to help. At the time, this particular staff member was doing well, but needed something to get him going again. He had grown bored and needed a challenge. I gave him the authority to meet with different companies and begin playing with layouts and types of equipment we would need. He came alive again! Giving him the authority to make decisions caused him to re-engage on a deeper level in his role. When you empower others to do something, you are helping them grow and develop. With new growth comes fresh levels of engagement.

2. **Enjoyment** – Empowering your staff increases their enjoyment

and job satisfaction. Give them credit. Share the spotlight. Let them take pride in the work they have done and relish the accolades. Leaders should aspire to create environments where people enjoy their jobs and look forward to coming to work. When you empower those around you, the work environment improves. Improving the staff's overall level of enjoyment increases their individual creativity and their personal standards of quality.

3. **Equipping** – My dad took me fishing from time to time. I loved every second of it. My dad would provide the fishing pole and line along with any needed bait, hooks and bobbers. He would do everything for me and once we got to a good fishing hole, he would simply put the pole in my hand and tell me to watch the bobber. All I had to do was pull up on the line when my dad told me to. When I did what he told me to, nine times out of ten I had a fish on the other end. Success! It was so much fun. The day came as I got older when my day started having me do all the set up on the fishing pole. At first, I had no clue what to do and it wasn't as fun with all the set up and work beforehand. Through repetition and practice I got it down and became pretty good at it. My father empowered me in fishing by teaching me to do it on my own. Leadership is about teaching your people to do it themselves. It will take effort and work on your part, but in the end you and your staff will be better for it. What staff member is looking to be equipped for a new challenge or skill? Is there anyone who would benefit from learning more about budgeting, organizing meetings, managing events, marketing, branding, or doing inventory?

Remember this as you begin: it likely won't be easy at first, and will take more time and investment than you expect. Staff growth and development is a gradual process. The old proverb "Give a man a fish and you feed him for a day. Teach a man to fish and you feed him for a lifetime"[20] applies here.

4. **Elevation** – Empowering someone to do something they have never done elevates their career. Years ago my wife and I visited Pikes Peak in Colorado Springs Colorado. It took us several hours to reach the summit, but man, was it worth it! What I remember most is the view on top of the mountain, but I also remember parts of the journey to get to the top. There were times it was scary, long, and steep. It felt like it would never end. What kept me going though was the goal of reaching the peak. Empowering others may not always be enjoyable and there will be times when the journey feels long, but remember you are helping them elevate their careers. When they reach the summit the view will be worth every second.

5. **Exit** – When you begin empowering your people, they will grow in confidence, stature, and ability. The drawback to this is they will get to a point where you will need to promote them, or they will leave for something bigger. When this happens, you have done your job as a leader. Empowering others leads to growth, and growth is a catalyst for change. If you have led well, change will be natural and welcomed.

CHAPTER 5

Crawl Before You Walk

"Tell me and I forget. Teach me and I
remember. Involve me and I learn."

Benjamin Franklin

Learn by Doing

High school biology was not my favorite. In addition to an hour-long lecture every day, I had to attend a lab weekly for a three hour block. What can you possibly do in a biology lab for three straight hours? After attending a couple of labs, I realized the time flew by. The lab was structured to coincide with whatever chapters the teacher was lecturing on. To my surprise, I looked forward to attending the lab. The day we dissected a frog and examined its anatomy was invigorating and exciting. I would sit in the lecture and fall asleep from boredom but when we got to the lab and applied what we learned, I was brought back to life.

Leadership works in a similar way. We can read books on leadership, attend courses, and listen to lectures. We can watch others lead and hear testimonies of the lessons they learned over the years. We can seek out mentoring and sit at the feet of some of the most wise, seasoned, successful people but until we actually do something to apply it, we won't grow to our truest potential. Leading requires doing. You need a class room and you need a laboratory. You need a place to learn all about the nuances of what it takes to lead, then you need a space to try it out. The best way to learn to lead is by doing. One of my favorite sayings from coaching says "Repetition is the mother of skill".[21] In other words, if you want to be really good at something and develop a skill you have to put the reps in. Skill requires practice. In your leadership journey, you need to get your reps in. You need a laboratory. You need to find a place or position you can practice and learn by doing. Let's look at five ways you can grow in your leadership and learn by doing:

1. **Volunteer Positions** – If you don't currently have a leadership position, don't wait for it. Find an organization where you can volunteer to lead. Signup to be the team mom for your daughter's soccer team, or run for chair president at the humane society. Going on a missionary trip to oversee a building project for needy families. Leadership isn't learned in a vacuum. Any position or place where you can volunteer and lead others will pay dividends to your growth.

2. **Boards and Councils** – Every town has a city council and every school has a board; both of these organizations are always looking for someone to step up and lead. You may not get the position you want and it might be inconvenient but it will be better than having to wait for something to fall in your lap. Be creative in how you think about learning leadership. It doesn't

always have to have some big title or position. Sometimes the best leadership can be learned from a position of minimal power or influence. Earn your leadership stripes by serving and paying your dues. Leadership is learned daily, not in a day.

3. **Join Toastmasters**[22] – One of the best professional growth opportunities I learned leadership from was joining a Toastmasters Club. Toastmasters International is a non-profit professional club that is known for helping improve personal communication skills. They also have a leadership development component to it as well. Each club has different roles and positions you can sign up for depending on what area you want to grow in. Additionally, the Leadership Development Program has different levels you can work through ranging from mastering fundamentals, time management, implementing a plan, and leading a team. The club is affordable and allows you to work at a pace that is flexible depending on your availability.

4. **Coach a Team** – Leadership is all about working with others. When you coach a team, even if it's your son's little league baseball team your leadership acumen will soar. Your communication and ability to problem solve will improve. Dealing with losses, unhappy parents, and figuring out the different motivation styles will pay dividends down the road as a leader. Though coaching a team may not be your dream job or position, it can be a great place to test your leadership skills.

5. **Start a Side Business** – If any of the above don't float your boat, start something on your own. Many aspects of starting a business can be very beneficial to your growth as a leader. Drawing up a business plan, branding, marketing, budgeting,

hiring staff, getting feedback, and serving customers all are skills that can sharpen your leadership. At the end of the day, all great leaders are catalysts. They make things happen. When you start your own side business, you are making plays and not sitting around waiting for your ship to come in. Swim out to it.

Today more than ever we need more "laboratory" settings for leaders. Those places where leadership isn't just taught, it is caught. Lectures, podcasts, and courses are great but where the rubber meets the road is in actually doing something. The day I took the scalpel and cut into the frog's underbelly to examine all the organs with my hands, my learning went to a whole new level. As you continue to improve your leadership, search out places and positions where you can get your reps in. Listen to lectures on leadership but whatever you do, don't skip your lab. It is there you will learn the most by doing.

Bringing Others with You

Growing up in the south, one of our big family traditions was our summer vacation. We either traveled by station wagon, like the Griswold's, or minivan depending on the year and what we could afford. If you have ever had the pleasure of traveling with a large family in tight quarters for days' long road trips and staying in cheap hotels with few to no amenities, you have experienced life on a whole new level. One of these trips requires the patience of Job and, with so many people, it is *always,* and I mean always, an adventure. As one of the oldest siblings of six children, my duties and roles were constantly evolving to meet my parents' needs at the time. When I was younger I was my dad's assistant, loading and unloading luggage from the large rack attached to the top of our station wagon. As I got older, I became the referee between siblings who got on each other's nerves, and was instructed to sit between them to keep them from assassinating each other. Somehow, we arrived at our destinations alive and in one piece!

As a leader, you will have to accomplish a mission. To do this, you will need to get really good at taking others with you. Anybody can do something alone, but the best leaders are great at bringing others with them. Like our vacation journeys in my youth, it is never easy, not always fun, and most often takes much longer to arrive at the destination than if you traveled alone. The work can be very taxing, but when done right, with perspective and patience, it can be some of the most rewarding work you will ever do as a leader. Let's look closely at five of the biggest challenges of bringing others with you.

1. **Not Everyone Will Want to Go** – Once you decide on your mission and cast a vision for the future, you might assume everyone will be able to see the bigger picture, and be just as excited as you. Like vacationing, not everyone is excited about going and they probably aren't looking forward to the long drive. You will need to determine if they do not want to be uncomfortable, or if they are not supposed to be on the bus with you. It falls to you to discern who should be on board with you.

2. **It Will Take Longer with More People** – The more people you have on board, the longer you will need to get where you are going. Our vacations were never short with such a large family. We had more restroom stops, meals took longer, loading and unloading the car took time, and finding hotels that could

sleep large numbers was next to impossible. On top of that, we naturally experienced more conflict and relational stress than most. This made vacation challenging and also took away some of the fun. Keeping the difficulties and inconveniences in mind will help you handle issues as they come up. Create a timeline for accomplishing your mission but always know it will take longer than you anticipate.

3. **Relational Conflict Is a Guarantee** – Conflict is a natural part of life, especially when you are trying to accomplish something significant. Dealing with conflict can save you time, money, and resources. When you avoid difficult conversations and avoid addressing relational tension hampering your journey, it not only has the potential to derail you as a leader but those on your team will pay as well. If conflict is not dealt with, toxicity can set in and the culture can quickly go bad. No culture is perfect but unresolved conflict can ruin and sour the mission. Any time you deal with relational stress that is keeping you from working on real problems, you experience sideways energy. Sideways energy can rob you of momentum and cause you to stall. Avoiding relational tension as a leader sends the message that you lack the commitment and conviction to the importance of the mission. Stepping up, addressing these difficult issues not only saves you a lot of headaches down the road, it frees up time and energy to cover ground more quickly towards your goals and objectives.

4. **Adjusting Your Route** - If you have ever been on a cross country road trip, you know there is always a detour, accident, or road closure of some sort. Today we have GPS to help us reroute

quickly and get us back on track. In leadership, the ability to adjust and find creative ways around problems is a must. Do your best not to panic or get too discouraged. Take a breath, sleep on it, and speak optimism into those you are leading. Leaders are dealers of hope. Whenever you turn negative or have a "give up" attitude, your attitude will be transferred to your staff. Even if you may feel that way on the inside, work to stay positive and see the good. Often, it helps to have a close associate you can lean on for a fresh perspective. Stay in the fight, take baby steps, and focus on small wins. Doing so will help you keep your head up and not throw in the towel. Find a way to win.

5. **Shut It Down** – Unfortunately there will be times when you will need to shut it down. Not doing something right now does not mean never, it just means waiting for a better time. Typically, this happens because of extreme situations like we experienced during the COVID-19 pandemic. Everything came to a screeching halt, and we were forced to toss the goals and plans we had in mind. At other times, it may not be the right season to do something. Timing is a critical component to success. You can dream, plan, and work towards your mission but if the timing isn't right, it can fail. Things to consider for good timing are political climate, budgeting, staffing, alignment with organizational goals and strategy, and your personal life. Never forget that your personal home life matters when considering the timing of a major decision. Any wise leader knows accomplishing something significant will be stressful on you. In other words, your family will feel it too. Having a

strong and healthy home life will be a haven where you can retreat to recharge and balance as you deal with problems and carry the weight of your mission.

The saying "It's lonely at the top" is a myth. Leadership can be lonely but it doesn't have to be that way. You can bring others with you. A journey of any kind is always better with companionship. It may not always be fun, and there are likely to be problems, but it is well worth it! The memories, experiences, lessons learned, and places you will see cannot be matched if you travel alone. Look at your leadership up to now. Are you someone who isolates themselves and intentionally leaves others out? How has it gone for you? Could it be better? Could you accomplish more? It's great to accomplish big things but it's even bigger to help others accomplish great things with you! If you are a leader who has been lonely, I encourage you to rethink your approach today. The next mission you take, invite others to travel with you. Bring them on board and buckle up!

Building a Team

I hated picking teams for playing dodgeball in elementary school. I was short and tubby, and not accepted by any of the popular kids in school. Peer dynamics being what they are at that age, recess dodgeball could get ugly. I was always one of the last to be chosen. After several games, however, I began to prove I was hard to get out. I stood my ground, and caught the fastest, hardest throws from the best players. I was determined to show the other kids I was no slouch and went from being picked last to one of the first selected. If I was on your team, I was determined to win!

When you find yourself in charge of building a team, it is not like elementary school dodgeball. Often, you will not have a say in selection. You may get paired with individuals based on the directives of others and they may not be the talented or motivated person you might hope for. You will have to find a way to work with those you find incompatible or have minimal rapport with. In her book *Team of Rivals*[23] Doris Kearns Goodwin discusses how President Abraham Lincoln found himself with a presidential cabinet he would not have chosen. Many were adamantly against him, yet President Lincoln had to work with his teammates to accomplish the greater good for society. At some point in your leadership journey, you will have to do the same, especially when building a team. Let's look at five principles for building and leading teams today:

1. **Build Your Team with Diversity** – Don't just hire those like you. The more diverse you can make it the better off you will be. If you are an all-male staff, hire a female. Or if your staff is all female, hire a male. Some of the best leaders are women in a male-dominated field, a strong female on staff will make you and everyone else better. If you don't have any minorities on staff, make a priority to change that. Additionally, recent research from Harvard Business Review reveals the more diverse your team is, the more innovative the group will be.[24] There is inherent diversity which involves traits you were born with (gender, ethnicity, and sexual orientation) and acquired diversity which are traits you gain from experience. Working in a different country can help you appreciate cultural differences or working with the opposite sex can give you gender smarts. Companies that have what they refer to as 2-D (inherent and

acquired) diversity unlocks innovation where "outside the box" ideas can be heard.

2. **Build Your Team with Good People First** – When you build a team, don't just look at talent and gifting. First and foremost, seek out good character. Are they caring, honest, thoughtful, and considerate? I don't care how good they are at what they do, if they do not treat others well, they will erode the chemistry and morale of the current team you have now. You must hire a teammate with a high level of competency, but they should be a good person with values compatible with the team. One question you can ask yourself is this: Would you invite them to be a part of your natural family? If not, then why would you add them to your team? Though they are not your family, they will be spending more time with you at work than you do your family. Make sure they are someone you would allow into your own family as well before you bring them on your team.

3. **Build Rapport with Team Members You Don't Get Along With** – There will be times you don't get along great with a team member and you cannot get rid of them. You didn't select them and you didn't hire them. You just got the command to work with and manage them. I will let you in on a little secret. You can either bite the bullet and find ways to work with them amicably or you can have a bad attitude towards them and make your life miserable. I have tried both and trust me, it makes your life and theirs much easier if you seek to find common ground, work to build trust and rapport with them, and build a bridge. Make a consistent effort to work with people you may not like or get along with. The beautiful thing about building

a team is that in the process you are changed, challenged and stretched as a leader.

4. **Build a Team of Rockstars** – If the team you have isn't working, make some changes. Don't settle for a team of ho-hum, unmotivated people who are not getting the job done. Have crucial conversations with people about their job performance. Calling others up to higher levels is uncomfortable for you and them, but if you avoid doing so, you can't be upset when the team doesn't perform. Sometimes making a change with one person on your team will radically raise the morale of your team. You cannot underestimate the negativity and drag a lack luster team member can have on other staff. It's like driving your car some distance without realizing your parking brake was on. Releasing the brake gives you a boost in power and momentum. Give the bad apple a time frame to improve for the better or make the change.

5. **Build a Team of Teams** – In his book *Team of Teams*[25], General Stanley McChrystal details how he restructured the army during the war in Iraq. At the time, the US Army was siloed, spread out, and heavily bureaucratic. This had worked in the past but the enemy they faced in Iraq moved fast and changed daily. If the US military was to find success, General McChrystal would need to make some changes. The Team of Teams is a term he came up with in a different way to lead and build teams. In the traditional style of leadership, it was a top down approach. One man led and everyone else followed under his command. In a Team of Teams approach, teams would be fluid and interconnected. On some days and on certain missions,

I might lead. On other days and in new challenges, someone else would lead and I would follow their leadership. In the end, building a team is about winning and finding a way to get the mission accomplished. When you lead teams today, you have to get rid of the top down command and control style. If you want to build a great team and be successful, adopting a "Team of Teams" type of philosophy will only help you and those you lead.

CHAPTER 6
Staff Culture

"A culture is strong when people work with each other, for each other. A culture is weak when people work against each other, for themselves."

Simon Sinek

Take Plenty of Vitamin C

During cold and flu season, my Mom pumped us full of vitamin C. I can still hear her today, "Make sure you take your vitamins right now. It will boost your immune system and keep you from getting sick!" If I had a nickel for every time I heard that growing up I wouldn't have had to work after college. As I have gotten older now and have children of my own, I realize how right she was when I was a young boy. Back then, I chalked it up to nonsense and tuned my Mom out. Today, I have a different perspective and I want my kids to stay healthy.

I want to talk about staff hiring and how it connects to work culture. Just like vitamin C will protect and boost your body's immune system from getting sick, so the 3 Cs I will share with regards to hiring staff will help protect and keep your team healthy. Just like my mom cared for us as kids, in many ways you will need to look after and care for those under your leadership. The 3 Cs will help you do that. In my early experiences with hiring staff, I had no clue what I was doing. If you wanted to work with me and help out, I welcomed you with open arms. It didn't take me long to find out that wasn't a wise way to hire staff. I brought on more problems and headaches than I was ready for. When I started using the 3 Cs as a filter and guide for who I would look to hire, my chances of getting it right increased drastically. The 3 Cs are:

1. **Character** – As I mentioned earlier, anyone you recruit or hire must have good character. This will set the tone for how you do business and how you handle problems. The character of your staff will also dictate the kind of problems you might face. Humans make mistakes. When you deal with someone who has great character, the issues that arise are not as messy, and they get cleaned up a lot easier. When you hire someone with outstanding character, you don't have to worry about how they will act and behave when you are not around. What someone does when no one is looking impacts the quality of their work when everyone is looking. You cannot compartmentalize your work and private life. Today, more than ever, the lines have blurred. There are fewer ways to hide what you do when no one is around. If it's not right, it eventually will come out. Having employees and staff with good character will protect you from embarrassment or, at worst, litigation.

2. **Competency** – Equally important to character is competence.

Just like you need good character when no one is around, so too when the lights are up and everyone is looking you need employees who can operate competently. You can have good character but if you are not any good at what you do, nobody will want to work with you. You will spend more time cleaning up messes that shouldn't be occurring. Hiring competent staff is equally as important as hiring staff with great character, the two go hand in hand. To have one without the other is a recipe for disaster.

3. **Chemistry** – After you check the boxes of character and competence, look for chemistry. This can be harder to detect unless you have a chance to see how they interact with others. Bring in potential hires to meet everyone they will be working with. Create some official interview opportunities but, more importantly, create some time to let everyone talk and spend time together in a more relaxed setting. In doing so, you will get a better sense of what kind of person they are. Do they have a sense of humor? Can they relate to others on different levels and topics? Are they too uptight? Do they come across as abrasive? Are they awkward or too quiet? Do they have a life outside of work? All of these things matter when you start putting people together for long periods of time or when they are collaborating on a stressful project or deadline. If your staff cannot get along, they will not go along. Creating good staff chemistry and maintaining it will be key to your sanity and can boost your staff's morale over time.

Using the 3 Cs has seen some good success. Through mistakes and frustrations, I have learned there are a couple more filters needed to add to your interview process if you want to really be able to figure out who would be a great hire for you. In addition to the 3 Cs consider these two filters as well:

4. **Look for a Values Match** – I have found out you can check all the boxes on the 3 Cs and still miss on a hire. Someone can have good character, competency, and chemistry but still not be a good fit for you and your staff. The answer to this is a values match. Values are those areas of life where you hold strong inner belief and conviction. It's who you are. It's not a right or wrong thing, it's more like an internal compass that pulls people together. When you lack a values match, there is something missing and the new staff member will always seem unhappy. For example, if you have a staff that really values work life balance and the potential new hire doesn't like to take much time off, that is a values mismatch. They may have good character, competency and chemistry but because they don't value what your current staff does, it will not work out. Look for areas where your current staff matches with the values of any potential staff addition.

5. **Hire for Attitude and Train for Skill** – This is an addendum to the competency principle. When looking to fill a position, you will not always find someone who has everything. Often, those who are really good at what they do have years of experience and aren't always willing to adapt and change. Without realizing it, they lack the right attitude to get the job done. Ultimately, they can and will cause a lot of headaches if they do not have the right attitude. I have learned when looking to fill a position, hire for attitude and train for skill. If you find

someone with an exceptionally good attitude, and they are good enough at what they do that they could be really good with some time and training, do not let them get away. Offer them the job! When you have someone who has a phenomenal attitude and is maybe a little green on the job, you can work with them and bring them up to speed quickly. You will still have to deal with some issues but they will be small in comparison to the stress you will encounter with a hire who has a bad attitude.

Hiring staff is something you can get better at over time. Hiring people will be something you must mature in. It is not something you can just pawn off on others, nor can you take it lightly or rush the process. Paradoxically, your biggest problems will be dealing with staff and your biggest answers to problems will be dealing with staff. People can create or solve problems for you. Just remember my Mom's wisdom as you begin the process, "Take plenty of vitamin C". It may not keep you from getting sick but it will lower your stress levels and the headaches you have will be far and few between.

Staff Meetings

Meetings suck. Period. I cannot recall any meetings where I walked out and thought to myself, "That was fun". However, as a leader, you need to meet with your staff. I remember the day I got promoted to lead our department, and I wanted to start meeting consistently as a staff. In the past, my experience with staff meetings was mostly reactive, meaning something wasn't going right or needed to be addressed so we had to meet. I always went into those meetings with my heart rate elevated and my guard up. I knew if I wanted to be effective as a leader, I would need to figure out a better way to do meetings.

Over the years, I have tried several different ways to lead staff meetings. There may not be a right or wrong way necessarily, but let me provide some rationale and reiterate the importance of having regular staff meetings. As I look back over the years, I am thankful for staff meetings now. Though we haven't always enjoyed or looked forward to them, they helped us operate as a unit and provided cohesion we would not have had if we didn't meet. Let's look at five reasons to hold regular staff meetings:

1. **To Strengthen Relationships** – Regardless of the size of your team, one objective is to strengthen and bolster the relational bond between those who work under you. If you do not meet or get together, the relational glue will dry up. Simon Sinek's book *Leaders Eat Last*[26] addresses how our government officials struggle to get along today simply because they no longer live close to each other like they did in the past. There are no lunches together, side conversations in the office, rapport building, or support from each other because they aren't getting together regularly. Sinek argues that because our government officials no longer work near each other, they don't have good relationships and when they must discuss controversial topics it makes it harder to work together. Their time together has diminished over the years. Remember this: when you and your staff get together, you are creating opportunities for them to get to know each other better. Some of the interaction will be formal but, over time, it will grow more casual. Those little

deposits of time spent together will add up to a stronger, more connected, and closer team. Meet regularly.

2. **To Open Lines of Communication** – The primary goal of staff meetings is communication. If you never meet to discuss different things in your department, no one will have an opportunity to share their own thoughts and ideas. By meeting as a staff, you are opening the lines of communication. Topics like scheduling, budgeting, vacation days, how to handle policies and procedures, current updates on teams and projects someone is working on and if someone is struggling right now and needs help will surface because you opened the lines of communication. By holding staff meetings and creating an environment where everyone shares, even the quieter team members will open up and speak. Not everyone will be great at this and that is not the goal, but even the worst communicators can become better. When communication is cut off, abnormality sets in. It is so important to regularly meet as a staff.

3. **To Provide Direction** – Imagine taking a trip across the country and never talking to anyone in the car, or listening to a GPS for directions? How would that trip go for you? Leadership is similar, you need to provide direction and vision about where you are headed. Something as simple as giving updates will do wonders for you and your team. Questions come up in staff meetings about what is currently going on, how something needs to be addressed, or what are we supposed to do next. John Maxwell says, "People are down on what they are not up on".[27] It is so true. When others are aware of what is going on and have context for their work, they usually will be good with

it. Provide direction on what is going on and what is coming down the pike. Anyone can chart the course, but it takes a leader to steer the ship[28].

4. **To Increase Focus** – When you meet, have an agenda as this is crucial to avoid letting things slip through the cracks. The bigger the team and the more siloed you are, the easier it will be for things to fall to the side. In your agenda, assign different people to lead parts of the meeting, and go over any updates or progress being made on current projects. By doing so, you hold others accountable and, most importantly, you create boundaries to keep your department focused on what matters most right now. There may be items that arise in the meeting that need to be addressed that weren't initially on the agenda, but the agenda acts as a roadmap to effectively moving through the meeting and keeping everyone on track.

5. **To Provide Variety** – Over the years I have toyed with different types of meetings. Some have gone well and some not so much. The four most common I have tried and used most are:

    A. Daily huddle – this can be a short 5-minute meeting for a quick update, inspirational thought, or a check in on where everyone is at for the day.

    B. Weekly meeting – this meeting would need to be a little longer and typically is held at the beginning of the week. This meeting can last from 20-30 minutes in duration depending on what topics need to be discussed. Also, this meeting should have more depth to it and provide clarity on objectives for the week.

C. Monthly meeting – this is my favorite type of meeting. I am not always a fan of meetings, but a monthly meeting allows for consistency. This meeting typically should last about an hour. Sometimes it goes longer if we are discussing something more serious that requires reflection and feedback from everyone. Keep a set time limit so staff can look forward to it and can plan around it.

D. Yearly retreat – Although a retreat is the hardest to schedule, because of the nature of it, I block out anywhere from 4-8 hours. If possible, having this meeting off-site works best. This reduces distractions, interruptions, and anyone wanting to stop by because they are bored. A yearly retreat also requires more preparation: catering breakfast and lunch, sending out materials and agenda, solidifying guest speakers, or bringing in a consultant to lead your team through some exercises are all great ways to structure this meeting. Typically, the main purpose of this meeting is to reflect on the past year, look into the future and dream about what you want to achieve next. This can also be a time to develop your staff in an area that would benefit them most. Resume building, personal branding, project management, and vision casting are all great tools to use in a yearly retreat meeting.

No matter the format, style, length, or agenda you choose, start meeting more regularly. Not everyone will love it and some will dread it at times, but if you stick with it you will see your team grow relationally. As a leader, you will have a greater sense of where you are headed. Looking back over the years, I am thankful I started this discipline. I have witnessed other departments, who don't meet regularly, flounder because they have lost touch and connection. Whether we want to admit it or not, we all need each other in our work. The quality of relationships make a difference in our work lives. The best work environments have a culture of mutual camaraderie, respect, and consideration for each other. By meeting regularly, you will achieve this goal.

Getting Your Staff Outside Their Comfort Zone

We all love comfort. Nobody really enjoys doing something that makes them uncomfortable. I remember the summer we visited Disney World in Orlando. I was a teenager, and it was supposed to be magical. It was not. It was, in fact, a nightmare. For the record, I am not a fan of roller coasters. Never have been and never will be. This particular day, my baby sisters had a brilliant idea of riding Space Mountain, which was the coolest roller coaster around. You were barely strapped into a small cart and the ride plummeted into a huge, dark space. Up, down, sharp turn right, sharp turn left, straight drops down or loop-the-loops. My sisters ran like world class sprinters towards the line to enter Space Mountain, but I didn't budge. I had absolutely no desire to get on a fast, out-of-control roller coaster that zoomed in all different directions in the pitch-black dark. My dad shot me a warning look that told me he expected to get on that coaster if my sisters did. He grabbed my arm and literally dragged me to the entrance. I dug in both heels and acted like a baby: whining, resisting, and causing a scene. Despite the embarrassment, my dad won and I got on the ride. My heart was racing and felt like any moment it would jump out of my chest. I was petrified. My sisters were loving it, but I was enraged with fear and anger. My disapproval and disgust invigorated their joy as they laughed at me. To my surprise, I made it through the ride that day, even grudgingly admitting that I actually strangely enjoyed it. Years later as an adult, I willingly got on the same ride again and couldn't believe I was so scared as a young man. My perspective changed as I got older.

It is important to get outside your comfort zone. Not much growth happens if we are always comfortable. The powerful thing about discomfort is how it causes you to move and change. Without change there is no growth. If your staff never steps out of their comfort zone, they will always be the same. The day my dad forced me to get on Space Mountain altered my fear of getting on a roller coaster because I was forced out of my comfort zone. Each step outside of your comfort zone is an opportunity to expand your capacity in that area. What was terrifying before can become something attainable. Facing a fear can become a catalyst to give you confidence and courage to step out and try something new. Unlocking your thinking has the power to set you free to be all you can be. Let's look at five reasons why it's critical to get your staff out of their comfort zone:

1. **People Don't Jump Willingly** – Most people will not do something uncomfortable on their own. They need coaxing and a push. Baby eagles studied in captivity have been documented to not leave the safety of their nest even though they are strong enough to fly. If this happens, the mother will nudge their babies out of the nest in an attempt to get them to fly.[29] If they do not fly on the first attempt, she will swoop down, grasp them with her claws, and fly back up into the sky. Then, she drops them again. She will repeat this process until they flap their wings and fly on their own. The same is true for us.

We will not leave the comforts of our situation until we are forced to. We are capable of flying on our own but won't often try without a push.

2. **Increased Confidence** – Fear makes us hesitant. The first time I was our camp director in the summer, I was very anxious about taking on such a large task and responsibility. I wasn't sure what I had signed up for. I made it through, and while it wasn't perfect, it went much better than I expected. That summer filled me with this sense of confidence that I could do anything now. That one experience had a tremendous impact on increasing my confidence as a leader.

3. **It Will Help Them Mature** – Maturation is a process and requires some uncomfortable steps along the way. Maturing requires failure and learning from those mistakes. Sometimes, we learn quickly, though most of the time we learn the hard way after repeated mistakes. Either way, we still need to mature and grow, and growth doesn't happen in your comfort zone. In the moments your staff gets uncomfortable they will learn and remember. Getting them comfortable being uncomfortable truly takes time to develop. It will not happen from one experience or moment. It is a process that requires repeated intentionality.

4. **Learned Humility** – Knowledge and information is not the same as wisdom or experience. As a younger coach, I thought I knew it all and was capable of handling any situation or circumstance. I could not understand why my boss made such terrible decisions. I often believed I knew better. As I got older and was faced with similar decisions, I was repeatedly

humbled by the realization of how wise my boss actually was at the time. Finally understanding how hard it was to make those decisions, I ended up doing something very similar to my boss. Humility is so crucial for anyone wanting to lead. I sometimes call it "leading with a limp". If you have been humbled, you begin to realize that It's not all about you and you don't have all the answers. Being humble means you listen more than you talk. You ask questions more than you answer them. You make decisions more carefully because you want to make sure you walk in compassion.

5. **It's Fun** – Meaningful work needs to be memorable at times. Helping your staff out of their comfort zone will leave them with memories they will never forget. Just as adversity makes you stronger, times of enjoyment and fun bond you together. There will be seasons and times in your life as a leader, your staff will need to laugh. Laughter and joy are like medicine, good for the soul. Leading isn't just about getting things done, but also caring for people. When you genuinely care for others, you care for their entire being, not just what they can do for you. Never forget: a happy workplace is a productive and engaging workplace.

Keep in mind everyone has different levels of discomfort. Take care not to push someone so far they fail miserably and are embarrassed. The goal is to help them grow, not crawl into a shell and hide for the rest of their lives. Do some homework on how far you should push someone. The key will be to get them just outside their comfort zone little by little. Think of it like peeling an onion: take one layer off at a time. Growth is a gradual process and smaller steps have a bigger impact in the long run. If you do end up going too far, recognize it, own it, and apologize for it. Back up, learn from it and explain your intentions are only to help them develop and grow. Ask them if there would be a better way to approach it next time.

If you have someone who is consistently resistant to getting out of their comfort zone, you may need to intervene at some point. Never trying anything new or stepping out to take a risk at learning a lesson can be a red flag. Complacency can be a problem especially if it's a staff member who has been there awhile and had some success. I have found older staff members don't like to try new things, especially if it forces them to learn new ways, make new relationships or try new technology. If there is a staff member who is not budging, you may need to use some stronger coercion to get them to take the first step. They may not like it or enjoy it at first, but I truly believe if you have the right motive and intention behind it, they will appreciate your efforts in the end.

Who is Holding Your Ladder?

I am terrified of heights. When I was a young boy, I made a deal with my mom to paint the outside of the house one summer in return for a very expensive remote-control car. I worked out the details of the agreement with my step dad, and we shook on it. He bought the remote-control car that day and I immediately began painting the exterior of our house. The first couple of weeks were exhilarating. I played with my car for hours on end between painting portions of our house. Then came the day when my painting momentum came to a screeching halt. The house we lived in at the time was a two story with very high elevations in the center sides of the house.

Everything up to that point was no problem, but when I got to that part of the project, I stopped. For days on end, I didn't paint. In his frustration, my stepdad complained to my mom about me not finishing the house. He had held up his end of the bargain and I was failing on my end of the bargain. After a long talk, my mom told me, "Either finish it, or tell him you can't". I made the decision to hold up my end of the deal. There was one huge problem, however: we didn't own a ladder long enough to reach the center eves. Even with the ladder fully extended it wouldn't come close, and it was unstable for whoever was standing at the top. Given my fear of heights, there was no way I was going to climb all the way up that ladder, reaching with a paint brush to paint the eves of the house. After a bit of collaboration with my step dad, we determined the best way to get it done would be to back up his truck and angle the bed of the truck so the ladder would be tightly secured and stable with me on top of it. Now in retrospect, this may not have been the best plan of action, but the weight and stability of the truck gave me the confidence to make the climb and finish the remaining bit of painting I had left to complete. It was still super scary, but it allowed me to finish the paint job and get my mom off my back!

In many ways, your career is like climbing a ladder. The higher you go, the more you can see and do but you also face greater risks and dangers. It is crucial to ensure you have someone you can trust to hold your ladder steady as you climb. Failing to do so can cost you professionally. Your reputation, character, and future opportunities are at stake. Let's look at five traits of ladder-holders to look for as you climb professionally:

1.   **They Provide Perspective** – That day when I climbed the ladder

for the first time, my stepdad was talking to me and giving me feedback. He knew my fears, concerns, and hesitations about being up so high. I not only trusted him, I knew he wanted to see me succeed. His voice and input as I worked was critical. He kept me at ease and offered a perspective from the ground that helped me navigate the stress of being suspended twenty plus feet above the earth.

2. **They've Got Your Back** – At the end of the day, your ladder-holder wants to see you succeed. They do not want to see you get hurt, or fail. This is someone who you know intimately, and have witnessed their true character in many different scenarios. How do they personally handle their problems and crises? Do they hold similar values as you do? How have they treated others in the past? Are they more opportunistic and self-serving or do they like to help others succeed? Seeing someone's track record over time is essential to your career welfare.

3. **They Know and Understand You** – Your ladder-holder doesn't need to be your best friend, but they do need to know you. By that, I mean they know your strengths, weaknesses, fears, concerns, and habits. My step dad knew who I was and he knew I could do it even when I didn't think I could. By knowing me, he was able to coach and guide me as I went higher and higher. If something wasn't right or if he detected too much anxiety and uncertainty in me, he would ask me to come down and we would start over. Every single time he did this, it helped ease my worries and gave me the confidence and

assurance to proceed. Your ladder-holder must be the same. They must know you and understand how you tick.

4. **They Provide Stability** – Every ladder has the potential to become unstable if not positioned correctly or not properly locked in place. Great ladder-holders will give you the stability you need to climb. Getting promoted and moving up in your career creates a lot of uncertainty and instability at times. Having the right person on the ground for you will give you stability to learn the job, make progress, and adjust along the way. Just like higher ladders need more weight at the bottom to keep it from moving, so the higher the stakes involved for you the more stability you will need.

5. **They Help You Find the Right Wall** – One of the most important jobs of a ladder-holder is to make sure you are leaning against the right wall. Sometimes, you can have the correct goals, and be aiming for the perfect target but if your ladder is leaning against the wrong wall, you will fail. That day when I was climbing the ladder for the first couple times, my ladder wasn't positioned in the right spot. My stepdad had to tell me to move my ladder to the right or left at times. I was leaning against the wrong part of the wall. It was amazing how small, subtle adjustments helped not just keep me safe but positioned me to do my job with ease and great success. Find an older mentor or a more seasoned colleague who can help you adjust and ensure your ladder is leaning against the right wall.

Though I may not enjoy climbing ladders with my aversion to heights, I do enjoy climbing the corporate ladder. Getting promoted is great but if you don't have someone holding your ladder, the fall can be devastating. You ask any successful leader, and you will see they had someone in their corner helping and holding them up. Who you select to hold your ladder can literally be the determining factor to how high you climb! Choose wisely.

CHAPTER 7

Investing In Your Staff

"You don't build a business, you build people,
and then people build the business."

Zig Ziglar

Mentoring is a Must

Leadership is a lot like parenting. Parenting requires a lot of effort to raise good kids. Left on their own, kids don't tend to do too well: they make poor choices, hang with the wrong crowd, and only think about the here and now. However, children with parents who pay attention and care about what's best for them have a shot at growing up and being responsible adults.

In 2001, Karen and I had our first baby girl, Isabel. We were such excited and proud parents. We were going to raise our little angel right! She would be respectful and responsible, and a woman of character (which she is today, by the way). Man, were we naive. It was harder than I could have imagined. She didn't always obey, didn't always do things exactly how her mom and I wanted, and marched to the beat of her own drum. No matter what we did to "force" her into being this perfect person, it just didn't happen. She is now a young adult, navigating her own way through life, and I'm realizing she changed us more than we changed her. Through the years, Karen and I grew more patient, more compassionate, understanding and loving.

You think you know how to parent until you bring that sweet little angel home and then you question everything. You can take classes, read books, and listen to podcasts on parenting but until you actually parent a child, you never really know how. Leadership is similar. You can read books, talk to other leaders, and take all the classes in the world on leadership, but until you start leading someone, you will not know how to lead. This is why mentoring others is essential for leadership! Mentoring someone is much like parenting. You come along with someone in a supportive, caring way to help them grow, learn, and mature. If you want to be a great leader one day, mentoring is something that will help you consistently improve. Just like Karen and I learned more from our kids about parenting in those early years than they did from us, being a mentor will do the same for you. Mentoring will do so much for you in regard to learning how to lead and oversee people than any podcast or class you could ever take. Let's look at five reasons why mentoring is a must if you want to get better at leading people:

1. **It's the Greatest Gift You Can Give** – The way you spell love is T-I-M-E. Whenever you give someone your time, you are telling them they matter to you. It is the greatest expression of value you can ever give. When I make time to visit with an intern or a younger coach to mentor them, it has the biggest and most positive impact. Recently, I was working with an intern and

helping him grow in the area of professionalism. He is very young, smart, and has a bright future but has some areas he needs to come up higher in. At first he didn't fully hear what I was saying but gradually, he realized the importance of it and started to improve. Though it took some time, mentoring made a difference. Pour into those you care for and see potential in.

2. **The Soft Stuff** – The greatest leaders know the soft stuff is the hard stuff. By "soft stuff" I am referring to having soft skills or good people skills. Being relatable, a good listener, approachable, and someone who others enjoy working with are the soft skills needed to be able to relate and connect with others. Some leaders are more naturally gifted in this area, but most have to invest time and practice to get better at it. Those of you who want to be great leaders one day, put yourself in positions where you can grow in this area. You can do this from either observing someone who is good at it; a boss or mentor. Or you can look for jobs where being more relational is required.

3. **It Gives People Life** – Mentoring is pouring your life into theirs. Lessons you have learned, mistakes you have made, and setbacks you have overcome will help give life to the person you are mentoring. It gives them hope that they are not a failure and provides perspective of what potential lies ahead. Like a good parent, when you mentor someone you have a chance to speak life into someone younger than you and provide them with a source of encouragement they cannot get from anywhere else. The best leaders don't just mentor, they give others life!

4. **You Learn to Lead with Grace** – Grace is having an ability to adjust your style and approach depending on who you are leading. If you have ever witnessed great parents with a bunch of kids, you will see this in action. It is a thing of beauty to see how parents with multiple kids can manage all the different personalities, moods, likes and dislikes, gifts, and talents, as well as shortcomings. Mentoring will teach you how to lead like this more than any other thing you will do. When you mentor, you have to learn different styles of motivation, communication, listening, and correction. No two people will respond the same to how you mentor them. Like parenting, it will be you who has to adjust and learn, not just the mentee.

5. **It Is the One Way You Can Give Back** – The best leaders are those who give back at some point in their journey. They took what they learned and gave back to others coming behind them. Today more than ever, we have so much information on the internet and unlimited courses you can take, and it is multiplying daily. However, we are losing the human touch. When you mentor, you are giving back and teaching younger leaders things they cannot learn off the internet or in a certification. They have tons of information today about what the business is but not much on how to do it. Younger leaders today need mentoring the most and the single greatest way you can give back is helping someone coming behind you.

As I look back over my 30 year coaching career, some of the most challenging and yet rewarding times have been from mentoring. Mentoring has helped me grow in areas I couldn't have learned any other way. It has brought me such joy and a sense of significance as

I have been able to watch younger mentees walk into their callings. Watching someone struggle and fail, but then get back up and dust themselves off to get back in the game has been empowering. As a mentor, you will help guide, encourage, equip and prepare others for the rocky road that lies ahead. The beauty comes when they persevere and get to the point where they are confident with themselves and find the courage to spread their wings and fly on their own.

Praises and Raises

They say the bookends of success are starting and finishing. If that's true, then praises and raises are the bookends of success when it comes to recruiting, developing, and retaining talent. Dealing with difficult employees can be very stressful, and retaining talented team members equally so. If you have ever lost someone on your staff who was very good at what they did, you felt it when they left. They leave a big hole. Filling that position can be very tricky depending on who is on the hiring panel. If you don't take care of your staff, especially those who do a great job, they will eventually leave you. They will look for a better job or someone will headhunt them. Be proactive in taking care of your people.

Think back for a moment about your previous jobs. Who did you consider a good boss? What did they do to make you feel that way about them? Who did a poor job as your boss? How did they treat you to make you feel that way? I would guess most, if not all, the bosses you liked showed you respect and care even when you made mistakes. The words they used, the tone, posture, and timing of what they said to you made you better. On the other hand, what was it the bad boss did that made you feel that way? I suspect they either overlooked you or failed to treat you in a way you felt valued. Those can hurt the most sometimes depending on the situation. Not giving credit, not acknowledging, and not showing respect can stay with you for a long time. Not only that, but it also makes you not want to do a good job for your boss. To be clear, I am not saying you can't get on someone or correct someone for not meeting expectations. Unfortunately, most leaders are great at pointing out where others failed or made a mistake. That is the nature of being a leader. You give feedback, hold others accountable, and call staff members up higher to ensure improvement. I get it. If you are going to be great at that, you must be just as good at pointing out when a staff member does something right. You don't have to do it every single time, but it needs to be consistent. As a leader, I challenge you to take inventory of your words with your staff. How often do you speak well of them? When was the last time you caught someone doing something right and praised them for it? In your staff meetings, do you always just focus on what is lacking? If so, you are treading on a slippery slope. You are sending a message that nothing is ever good enough, and low morale is right around the corner. If nothing is ever good enough, then why put any effort in to improve it. Be strategically and intentionally lavish with your praise where it is needed and deserved. Do not hold back. If someone is busting their butt, working long hours with a good attitude, dealing with tough situations and handling them with ease, tell them you see and appreciate it. Thank them for it.

The other way to show your staff they matter and how much you value them is by giving them a raise. When you give someone a raise, you impact their lifestyle and livelihood. You increase their pay. You give them more money for the time they invest at work.

Simply put you are saying to them, you matter, and we see the effort you are putting in. If they are doing a great job for you and you don't give them a raise it can leave a bad taste in their mouths. It sends a message that the work they are doing isn't valued. Great employees not only need to be rewarded financially to show their worth, but it also lifts the level of those they work with. Giving raises can have a ripple effect positively and negatively. You aren't always able to give everyone a raise at the same time or level, and that is part of leading others too. However, do what you can when you get a chance to do it. If you have a staff member who is underpaid and underappreciated, fight like crazy to get that fixed. Do all you can to not only retain them, but make sure you do it in a way that makes them feel good too. I have seen and experienced when you do it wrong and the person receiving the raise doesn't feel good about it. Anytime and I mean anytime you give someone a raise, they should walk away feeling positive about it. Too little of a raise depending on the situation can dishearten them. Negotiating too much and making them fight for it too hard can leave them beat up emotionally and not valued. A raise should be a reward, not an occasion to leverage and nickel and dime someone who is a great employee. Make sure they feel valued and celebrated when you give them a raise. It not only goes a long way, it lasts for a while. Use that to your advantage.

Let's look at five reasons you need to give praises and raises for your staff:

1. **It's What People Like Most** – If I wanted to make you happy, I would take you to your favorite restaurant. I wouldn't eat at a place you hated. I know without a doubt that if I took you to your favorite restaurant, you would be delighted. Not only

would you feel good, but you would probably even like me more. It's the same with praises and raises. Employees love it. I have never in all my years ever heard someone say, 'I am just way too encouraged around here'. 'You gotta stop with all the positive feedback, it's just too much'. On the other hand, I haven't ever heard someone say, 'They are paying me too much money for my job'. 'I can't take it; you need to lessen my salary'. You know why you haven't ever heard this, it's because they love it. Whether they will admit it or not is one thing, but rest assured it is the secret to building and keeping a great staff.

2. **It Reinforces Good Behavior** – When it comes to leading people, you ultimately are trying to change and reinforce good behavior for the better. Any negative, low performing behavior must be minimized or done away with and rewarding good behavior and habits will get repeated over time. Every employee is a little different and you may need to do some homework on what different staff respond best to, but make no mistake about it, what you reward will get repeated good and bad. Make sure you reward good behavior if you want to see it consistently done again.

3. **You Create a Work Culture Employees Enjoy** – Having a work environment and job where you can move up, grow, and show you are making a difference creates a culture of employee engagement. So many people today just go to their jobs and go through the motions for a paycheck. By being a leader who gives praises and raises, you create a work culture people love to work in. It is nice to be rewarded monetarily with a raise, but affirmations reward the desire of achieving a higher purpose

and significance. Always keep this in mind, one of the greatest motivators is a sense of purpose. When you praise someone for their work, intentionally connect the job they are doing and give them credit for the bigger picture of success you are experiencing. This in turn creates a work culture where not only are people valued but they are recognized and honored for a job well done. By doing this, if someone leaves it's not because of something you haven't done. It may just be time for them to go.

4. **Leaders Eat Last** – In Simon's Sinek's book "Leaders Eat Last" he talks about how in the military great leaders always make sure all the soldiers under their care get to eat first. After those under their care eat first, then the leader eats last. The true mark of a great leader will always be how he prioritizes and takes care of those under their care. If every time a raise comes up and you choose yourself over your staff, in my opinion you are a self-serving leader. You are using your staff to serve yourself. I am not saying you shouldn't ever get a raise. You should. However, do you take better care of yourself than you do your staff? How is their livelihood? Are they working extra jobs to get by? Don't be the guy who is thriving while your staff is scraping by. Leaders eat last. Take care of your staff first, then yourself last.

5. **Leave a Legacy** – As you continue to lead people over the years, you will begin to accumulate lives you have touched and helped along the way. Sometimes, it doesn't go well. You will mess up and make mistakes for sure. Just make sure as you go, you leave a legacy of people you have helped advance in their careers,

impacted their lives for the better, and taken them places they couldn't have ever reached on their own. When you look back, my hope is there will be a countless group of people you have influenced over your career. That will be the tell-tale sign of if you have been successful or not. When your time is up, who did you invest in and develop that is thriving because of your leadership? Being a leader who gives praises and raises will have that kind of impact over the long haul. At the end of the day, you have the opportunity to show people how much you care through your leadership and if you really want to leave a legacy as a leader you have to look out for your people.

There have been two times I experienced the impact of praises and raises in my own life. The first was my defensive line coach at Georgia, Steve Greer. It wasn't my job per se, but he praised me for my efforts and made me want to run through a wall for him. During my freshman year of football at the University of Georgia I was struggling at my playing offensive line. My coach was very negative and critical with his feedback on how I was playing. It felt like I could never do anything right. No matter what I did, good or bad, he criticized me. I considered quitting because it was so bad. One day out of the blue, Coach Greer asked if I would ever be open to changing positions to the defensive line. I lept at the chance for a fresh start. Coach Greer was hard on me and corrected me when I messed up but he also praised me when I did something good. It made all the difference for me. I not only ended up starting on defense, but finished my career and got my degree. To this day, I still am living on the impact of him encouraging me in a season of my life when I wanted to give up and quit. His words gave me life. The second pivotal moment where I felt the direct benefits of "praises and raises" came when I was promoted as director of athletic performance for Olympic sports at the University of Texas. The promotion changed my career path positionally and financially. The years of hard work and sacrifice finally paid off. Receiving that promotion and getting elevated not only helped me but it changed my family's life and those under my leadership.

Evaluations and Feedback

I walked into the weight room one day excited, acting goofy, and over the top. I was in a great mood. As I entered the room, my boss at the time, Coach Jeff Madden, was speaking with a guest. I walked up to them acting silly, dancing, and animated. Coach Madden stopped me, pulled me aside, and introduced me to our guest. It was none other than Michael Johnson, the Olympic Gold medal sprinter. Surprised, I extended my hand to introduce myself. I kept our interaction brief and carried on with my day. Later that day, Coach Madden pulled me in his office and gave some of the best feedback I have ever received. He told me to always carry myself professionally. The way I acted that day was not professional. His words stung, but I needed it. I hung my head and agreed with him. It was a wakeup call for me. The feedback was hard, but it was a teachable growth moment.

If you want to lead well, it will be critical to do what Coach Madden did for me that day. You will need to know not only how to give evaluations, but provide necessary feedback to those you lead. Evaluations are protocols and processes (both verbal and non-verbal) where you rate how an employee is doing at their job. It gives them a measuring stick of how their job performance has been up to that point. These are typically formal, but can be informal depending on the frequency you choose to do them. At some point during an evaluation, you will need to provide feedback to the employee. Feedback differs from an evaluation in that you are giving specific advice or counsel to the staff member on something you see that needs to change or improve. Evaluations tend to be a bigger picture of their overall performance, whereas feedback drills down into specific areas you as a supervisor want to address. Once you step into a leadership role, you are responsible for others. Your staff will be a direct extension and reflection of how you lead. You set the tone and example for those in your department, but providing authentic, honest, and valuable feedback will determine how much people develop under your leadership. Being able to evaluate and give feedback to your staff consistently and effectively will set you apart as a leader. Depending on what "ability gaps" your team might be lacking, whether it be professionalism, knowledge, skill competency, maturity, or even social intelligence; taking opportunities to provide necessary feedback during evaluations will help develop your staff and allow you to become a standout leader. Let's look at five principles on providing evaluations and feedback to help you invest in your staff:

1. **Be Observant** – If you don't take time to watch and listen, you will never have anything to say. Watch your people. Keep an eye on them. Pay attention to their dress, mood, follow-through on assignments, engagement, and their treatment of others. The more you pay attention to what your staff does, the more you reflect on how you are doing. Are you setting a good example? Are you portraying the attitude, dress, and work ethic you

expect of others? If not, you need to make some adjustments. Look in the mirror first. So many leaders today do not do what they say. They say one thing and do another. Double standards do not work. You can't expect others to do what you won't do yourself. Your staff will lose respect for you and become resentful. The feedback you provide won't be well received. Be a leader who buys what he is selling.

2. **Meet With Them** – After looking in the mirror, communicate with your staff. If you don't provide feedback they will never change. What behaviors are not ok with you? What habits need to change? Are there any attitudes or performance gaps? As you think through this and come up with a list of things to address, pick one or two things to discuss with them. The less you focus on, the better the chance of improvement. Be careful not to try and address too many areas at once and you end up getting little to no change. Select one or two areas you want to see improvement in and focus on those.

3. **Be Specific** – If you want to see effective change, be very clear and specific with them. Provide clear examples. For example, "When we were speaking last week, you kept checking your phone and I took it as being rude and disrespectful". They may not agree with you and may provide more context for why they were checking their phone, but now you have given them a specific example. Saying things like, "You lack focus" or "You come off disrespectful" or "You don't have good people skills" will not help them. General statements can come across as picking on them. Your main goal for providing evaluation and feedback is to see them grow and improve.

4. **Make It Routine** – To be effective, make evaluations and feedback a normal part of your work culture. If the only time you provide feedback is when something blows up, you will miss key opportunities to develop your staff. You can also run the risk of making these experiences negative. Evaluations and feedback shouldn't always be pointing out the bad or wrong an employee has done. They should also include times of encouragement and reinforcing good behaviors of what they are doing right. When you lay out a routine, change can be lasting and you will see your staff grow consistently over time. Find a good rhythm and timing that works best for you and your staff and stick to it. You are better off setting up specific times you can follow through on, versus trying to do too much and miss the mark.

5. **Get Their Perspective** – After you meet with them, give them time at the end to see what they think and if they have anything they want to say about your feedback. They may be upset, they may agree or disagree, or they may be shocked. No matter the reaction, it is important to provide time and space to allow them to respond. Doing so shows you care about them and provides you with a glimpse into their level of maturity and depth of character. It also allows you to see what they heard you say. Oftentimes, what you say to an employee can be interpreted differently than you meant it to be. Giving them a chance to talk and share their perspective with you will help you understand them and communicate better down the road.

Think through how frequently you want to do evaluations and give feedback. The more you do it, the more natural it will be for you and your staff. If you choose to do an annual evaluation, I recommend keeping a file on each staff member. Documentation throughout the year will support your ability to give an accurate evaluation. Quarterly assessments may be easier. If you choose to go this route and it's more frequent, you may not need to be as formal and paperwork heavy. Regardless of how often you decide, have a format and system you can stick with and one that gets good results. This will allow you to hold them accountable to the goals they have set and refocus as necessary.

When you do meet with people, take some time to consider your delivery. What tone do you want to have? Are you angry, frustrated, sad, disappointed, happy, or excited? How are they doing? Have they had a hard time in their personal life recently? Do they seem discouraged? Are they disengaged? These things should be taken into consideration. Your tone, body language, and the words you choose have power. Are they more sensitive? Do they need a more direct message? Are they too hard on themselves? Are they arrogant or cocky? How do you think they will respond? Be intentional about every aspect of doing an evaluation and providing feedback before you meet. It will dramatically impact your success during the meeting, and in future interactions. Do your homework with each staff member. Invest time and show you care.

Get Your Staff Ready for Their Next Gig

If there is one thing coaches live for and do on a consistent basis, it's getting their athletes and teams ready for the next big game, tournament, or season. Preparation is a way of life. Looking at where you are and figuring out where you want to go is critical to not just motivating someone, but you also need to plan out and prioritize for the coming days, months, and years ahead. The best coaches can see an athlete's future potential and lay out a plan to get them there. Like Michelangelo looking at a piece of unshaped marble, leaders have an ability to see the statue lying dormant within. With the right skill, a masterpiece will emerge. As a leader, you will need a similar mindset and approach with developing your staff as well. Plan and prioritize your staff's growth and development. If you don't, your staff will drift.

Helping others improve at their jobs, and finding greater purpose and satisfaction in what they do is one of the most satisfying things you can do as a leader. When you help someone change their life for the better, loyalty is achieved. You are always getting your staff ready for their next opportunity, and you should always be thinking how to get them ready. They may move on to bigger and better things, but never waste the opportunity to help your staff improve their skills and ability, even at the risk of them leaving. Dealing with someone who is unhappy at work, unengaged, or complacent is one of the hardest things to manage as a leader. If not dealt with, it has the potential to hold you back or drag you down. To help you avoid this, let's look at five ways you can help your staff get ready for their next gig.

1. **Set Aside Time to Meet With Them** – The main purpose of the meeting is to let them know you see great potential in them and that you would like to discuss ways to help them develop. Belief in people has the ability to raise them to new levels. It sends a message that you truly care about them as well as lets them know they have a future with the company. Expectations can be very powerful. It can be very motivating and encouraging. When you meet with them, make sure to

ask them questions to get their perspective. Ask them if they see this ability in themselves? Do they enjoy the current role they are in? Have they considered doing or trying something to help develop this talent or ability? People don't always see what they are good at. To begin the process of getting others ready, it's so important to see what they are thinking. This will help you generate ideas on first steps for them.

2. **Assign Them New Responsibilities** – If you see potential in one of your staff, give them new responsibilities. This can be anything from a special project, to overseeing an area of your department that needs attention, or even asking them to help in an area you are working on. A word of caution here: they may not be excited about this approach. It can be viewed as punishment or degrading if it's a job no one wants to handle. However, if you explain the opportunities that could arise from the newfound responsibilities, you are more likely to get buy-in from the start.

3. **Have Them Make a Professional Development Plan** – One of the best ways to get the ball rolling with your staff is to involve them in the process. Have them reflect and choose an area or two they really want to develop over the next six months or year. Once they have an idea, have them build a plan to grow in those areas. Perhaps they could take a class, seek out a mentor, read some books, or get certified in a new skill or specialty. Early on in my leadership development I found an affordable six-course certification on management and leadership that was flexible enough for me to complete without interrupting my work. The certification was instrumental for

my development as a leader. Development is not just about learning a new skill or gaining new information, but learning to think at a higher level. Leaders think differently than followers and getting your staff ready for promotion is all about changing the way they think.

4. **Let Them Fill In for You** – Invite them to lead a meeting or an event. Set them up for success by outlining your expectations and equipping them to do the job, while giving them freedom to execute. Find a good balance between giving them freedom to lead, while maintaining enough contact to keep a pulse on everything. Think of it like teaching a kid to ride the bike. Let them go, but stay nearby in case they get into trouble. Step in to help to get them back on track if needed, but then let them loose again and cheer them on! Allowing them to lead will develop confidence and maturity.

5. **Let Them Fail** – Embarrassment, awkwardness, and defeat are not qualities any leader likes to associate themselves with. Failure can be a great teacher, and can instruct on a deeper level than any course, class, or curriculum. The school of hard knocks remains one of the best degrees in life. Some never learn the lesson until they fail. When they fail, be there for them. Encourage them through the process. Walking your staff through a tough situation can help them grow as a leader if they will embrace it and learn the lesson. One word of caution here. Don't let them run from their mistake. If they run from it, they will never grow and are more likely to repeat the same mistake later on.

CHAPTER 8

Staying Grounded

"If you don't declare a finish line for your work, your body will."

Carey Nieuwhof

Avoiding Burnout

Our house caught fire in my senior year of high school. The house was still standing, though the front window was black and charred. Inside, the house was completely destroyed. One of the kerosene heaters had malfunctioned and caught fire in the living room. One of the neighbors saw smoke and called the fire department immediately. The fire had not leveled our house, but everything was burned out and good for nothing. The foundation was intact, and the frame of the house was undamaged but everything inside the house was ruined from the black smoke from the fire. My boom box had melted into a pool of plastic, and my clothes were black and crumbled like a dry leaf when I touched them. Everything had to be replaced.

As sad as that story is, I share it as an analogy for our careers. Our professions are much like houses. A house protects us, provides shelter, gives us great joy and relationships, and allows us to live a great life. However, it can be brought down in an instant and cause great loss. Burnout is something to watch for. So many leaders start off with passion, purpose, and enthusiasm but after years of working and fighting to get to a position you love and enjoy, burnout can sneak up on you and set in. Sometimes burnout builds slowly and other times it hits hard and fast. Everyone has different levels of stress and responsibilities and the rest needed to keep forging ahead will vary from person to person. Burnout is a result of being out of balance. Getting promoted often results in getting off balance by working longer and harder. At first, it is well worth it to get more money, better perks, power, influence, and status. One day, however, you wake up and realize you have lost your joy. Your drive and ambitions wane. You still are working but now it feels like a chore. When you experience this, you are entering into burnout, if you don't do something about it, the damage and recovery can take much longer than anticipated. Let's look at five strategies to help avoid burnout before it does too much damage:

1. **Take a Vacation** – American culture is horrible when it comes to taking time off. We love to work, work, work. It is ingrained into our society and heralded as a badge of honor. Taking a vacation does not mean take your work with you and work the whole time you are away. That isn't a vacation, it's working in a different location. The word vacation has at its root the word "vacate". It means to remove yourself and leave. A true vacation requires you to leave your work and city and go somewhere where you cannot be called upon or pulled on

for something work related. A recent study[30] commissioned by Apple Vacations polled 2,000 workers and found it takes most people on average 4 days to "switch off" from work and all the responsibilities, projects, and needs waiting for them. Staycations (staying at home) during time off may sound good but it is so easy to get sucked back into the rat race of work. When you take a vacation, you are giving your mind, body, and spirit a rest. Block your calendar, book the flight, reserve the hotel room, and make plans to get away to recharge and rest.

2. **Build Margin in Your Workday** – One of the biggest challenges stems from always being connected electronically. We are available all the time. No matter the time of day we can be contacted via text, call, email, or video. If we are not careful, we work hours and hours without ever looking up or taking a break. This may allow you to get more done and be productive, but really what you are doing is running yourself into the ground. Life was meant to be lived in rhythms. When all you do is go from one meeting to the next, you end up exhausted and worn out. As an example, could you imagine the world's strongest person lifting weights all day long never pausing for rest, water, and food? No, of course not. They would never get stronger that way. They achieve world class strength by pushing hard in bouts of intense exercise followed by prescribed periods of rest. They intentionally create margin to recover, fuel up, and go again. By doing so they can condition their bodies to go beyond normal boundaries of other humans. If you want to avoid burnout, work like a world class athlete. Build some margin into your workday. Clinical research published in

March 2021 at North Carolina State showed that employees benefited from "microbreaks". Occasional 5-minute breaks led to increased energy and likelihood of setting and achieving workplace goals.[31] Find a rhythm that works for you. Work for 2-3 hours and take a break. Go for a walk, run an errand, visit with a colleague, take a short nap, or read a book.

3. **Practice the 100 Hour Rule** – In the book, *Give and Take*[32], Adam Grant shares some Australian research on burnout from work. They found that those who volunteered at an organization outside of their work for two hours a week were significantly less likely to experience burnout. This is referred to as "the 100 hour rule". The power of volunteering allows you to get your mind off yourself and focus on doing something completely different for others. By taking time each week to get your mind off your work, you give your mind a break and lower stress levels. Making new relationships and contributing to the greater good, lifts your mood. Find a cause or a community you are drawn to. Research and find a way to get involved even if you don't have much time.

4. **Find Your "Third" Place** – Leonard Sweet talks about this in his book *The Gospel According to Starbucks*[33]. He says we can benefit from a "third" place in our lives. It's a place where you can build good relationships and experience a supportive community but you may not frequent it as often as work and home. A great example of this was from the famous sitcom series *Cheers.* If you ever watched the show, it always brought you back to the friendships and community the characters forged in the storyline. Drama, romance, conflict, humor,

and sorrow, the characters were intertwined. Though they didn't live together, the bar was the "third place" where they connected. Find a place you frequent consistently enough that you build relationships with people there. It can be a local coffee shop, a gym, hair salon, special interest group, or church. Time you invest there will lead to support, care, friendships, and a community to encourage you. When you do this, you are bringing balance into your life. You are taking time out for yourself and whenever you make yourself a priority, it is a good thing.

5. **Make Your Mental Health a Priority** – Carve out time to prioritize your mental health. Everyone has a bad day occasionally, but when the bad days turn into bad months or even a year, this is a problem. If you have been overworking and overextending yourself, and your mental health is taking the hit, you may need more than a week of vacation to address it. You may require some counseling to help rewire your thinking. Perhaps you need to change jobs or scale back your hours. Take a sabbatical. Stop and ask yourself how you are currently doing right now. What level of job satisfaction do you have? Are you lagging in motivation, drive, or inspiration? Has your work become drudgery? Is your mental health suffering? If so, these may be some warning signs of burnout. If you think you might be experiencing burnout, find someone who can help you figure it out. Small precautions now can save you years of defeat and set back. Don't keep putting it off either. The sooner you know what is going on, the better you will be in the long run. If you don't take care of yourself you will be useless to

those you care for. Life is too short, and work is never more important than your health and well-being.

Work Life Balance: The 5 Balls

I walked up to one of our head coaches one day working out on the stairmaster. After some small talk, he began to share with me the story of the five balls he had recently read. It was a picture of our life and how important our families are in contrast to all other aspects we deem important. Metaphorically, we all carry five balls. Four of them are rubber and the last one is glass. Each ball is symbolic of a different area of our life. Friends, hobbies, money, and work are the first four rubber balls. The last ball is glass and it represents our family. Four of the balls will bounce back if you drop them. You can get new friends, hobbies, and money. If you lose your job, you can find a new one. You will bounce back. However, if you drop your family, like the glass ball it will break. Though you may be able to put it back together, it will never be the same. As leaders we must be careful with how we handle our families. In your pursuit of a great career, don't let work consume you. Work life balance is almost cliché today. Leading requires a lot of your time and energy and if you are not careful, your family can be left out in the cold. I have personally seen this with leaders who have neglected their families at the expense of their job only to look back and feel the crippling pain of a broken marriage or estranged relationships with their kids. In the book, *The Top Five Regrets of the Dying*[34] by Bronnie Ware shares the second most mentioned regret from caring for the elderly was, "I wish I hadn't worked so hard". No one sitting on their deathbed thinks, "I wish I would have spent more time at the office".

You make time for the things that matter the most to you. If you get a new car, you keep it clean. If you purchase a ticket to go on a luxury vacation, you clear your calendar to take the trip. You plan, pay the fees, schedule the flight, book the sight-seeing tour, look up the directions and best route to the vineyard. Why? Because it matters. The same must be true for your family. If you really, truly love your family, you will make time. Talking about making your family a priority but never ever doing anything about it is lying to yourself and them. You may have intentions of being a family-oriented leader, but if you do not carve out time to be more present at home, nothing will ever change. If your default excuse is that you just don't have time, stop saying your family matters. They don't matter. You and your job are way more important than them. That might feel harsh but truth hurts when it hits home. As leaders, we work hard to hold others accountable and provide feedback but often when it comes time for us to look in the mirror and live what we preach, we fall short. We make excuses for working so much or keep kicking the can down the street with promises for tomorrow or the next day. Rhein Fathia says sometimes 'someday' means I know it will never happen"[35]. As hard as it may be to hear, it is true.

Make time for your family. Today there are so many who have passion and energy for their work and come home exhausted and checked out. We need to prioritize family first and build our work around those who matter most. John Maxwell defines success this way: "Having those closest to me, love and respect me the most."[36] To abide by this definition in our careers will require a longer career trajectory, but your family will be with you. They won't be left behind or neglected on the altar of success. Let's look at five ways you can protect your family and have a better work life balance:

1. **Set Boundaries** – Many leaders set a time when they will leave the office each day. Doing so sends a message that work isn't everything to you. The people you work with are important, but your family is more so. You have a life outside of the office. Not only that, but your family will also feel the love, care, and priority of how much they mean to you. The more time you have at home in the evening, the more opportunities you will have for meaningful conversations, creating memories, and helping with chores around the house. When you set a time to leave the office, family traditions, rituals, and routines begin to flourish. Two decades of research done by Harvard Graduate School has shown that families that make time even if for a few minutes to sit down, have a meal, and genuinely connect can improve the physical and mental health of those involved.[37] Set a time.

2. **Spend Time with Other Leaders Who Prioritize Family** – Find someone who lives this out in their life. Talk is cheap and a lot of leaders have wishbone when they need backbone. Don't spend time around others who always talk about doing this but never do it. Find a leader who walks the talk. Pick their brain, watch how they organize their work schedules, take them to lunch and ask how they have struck a balance between being a great leader at work and being a great wife, husband, or parent. I can guarantee you they have struggled with it as well and found some ways that have worked for them. Don't just always look for mentors in your work life, find some for your family life as well.

3. **Pivot Roles or Jobs** – Sometimes the easiest way to prioritize family is changing your role at work. Perhaps you need to unload some work off your plate. Maybe you need to start work earlier in the morning so you can get home at a decent time. It may even mean changing job titles and taking less money. Sometimes you may need to find a new job. Look for a supervisor who sees the value of your family, and how familial wellbeing relates to the quality of work you will do. All work isn't good work, and every job isn't a great job just because it pays a lot. Quality of life matters. The best leaders understand this, and seek to make sure their staff have a quality of life outside of work.

4. **Integrate Family into Work** – There will be seasons and times you cannot leave work early or change jobs. I have been there. You are locked into the season and the work life balance thing isn't even on the radar. One thing you can do though is what I call work life integration, and by this I suggest finding creative ways to bring your family into your work world. Set up a weekly lunch with your spouse. Find some windows of time when your kids can come to work with you. You would be amazed how happy your kids can be at work with you, even for a short time. I have had my girls come to my office and draw, reorganize, mess up, redecorate, and watch their favorite cartoons in my office for hours and they loved it. It's not ideal, but sometimes you must find ways to get small wins in life. The memories, interactions, and bonding you can accomplish by bringing your family to work will make a difference. It may

not always be convenient, but in the end the value of time with your family will be worth it.

5. **Get More Involved in Your Family's Life** – The only way you can really make any change is through commitment. Sign up to be the boy scout or girl scout leader. Be the team mom or PTA leader. Coach your son's baseball team. Carpool your kids to school every day. Be the chaperone for your kid's soccer team on tournament weekends. When you do this, you make a strong commitment to be around your family more. It also forces you to be more efficient at work, lean on your staff, and delegate more often. They will survive without you. Those emails will be waiting for you when you get back. Intentionally placing yourself in your family's activities will pull you in that direction naturally and backing out will be much harder when the most important people in your life are depending on you.

As you continue to grow as a leader and advance in your career, my hope is you will guard and protect the glass ball. After thirty years of coaching, I have yet to meet a leader who thought losing their family was worth it. Not even one. Every leader who has lost some aspect of their family carries regret and remorse. They typically express some form of ways they wish they would have done better. You don't have to be that person. If you can prioritize your family, you will not only lead well, but the legacy you leave behind will last for years after you turn in your keys. That, my friend, is the main reason we lead: to change and impact lives beyond our days. Let the rubber balls drop if you must but whatever you have to do hold tightly to the glass ball. Family matters most.

CONCLUSION
Disaster Relief

E arly one morning in February 2021, I woke up, walked into the living room and opened the blinds to a majestic sight I had never seen in over 20 years of living in central Texas. Large snow-flakes were falling to the ground and everything was covered in a sparkling white blanket from the night before. I stood in awe at the beauty of the scene because I had never seen so much snow in Texas. While it does occasionally snow in central Texas, the temperature rarely drops below freezing and if it does, it doesn't stay that low for long. In 2021, we experienced a record breaking storm that covered the entire state. The subfreezing temperatures lasted for days on end and the extreme cold resulted in widespread power outages across the state. Because many homes didn't have heat, pipes froze leaving people with no access to water. Infrastructure in the gas lines throughout the state failed and gas lines froze. Loss of electricity causing frozen pipes and gas shortages put a strain on the state's resources putting many people in dire circumstances. The damage from the storm made it one of the most costly weather disasters in the state of Texas, with repairs estimated to be at $1 billion. The two greatest needs during that eight day disaster were gas and water. Leadership also needs both figurative gas and water to survive. Every leader carries gas in one bucket and water in the other. You decide which to use based on the situation at hand, and if you choose not to use them, it will eventually cost you. You may not be going through a colossal winter storm that shuts down an entire state, but you must use what you have in your buckets to be an effective leader. If you are lacking vision and people are lacking motivation, stir them up with a fresh vision and challenge them. Don't water it down, light the fire! Gas can cause damage but used appropriately, it can fuel the flames and propel you into a season of excitement and adventure. Conversely there may be an instance where you need to stop a situation from going in the wrong direction, in this case, douse it with the proverbial water bucket. Use discernment and wisdom. A dose of kindness and empathy goes a long way. If people are running out the back door as fast as you hire them, ask yourself why. Maybe your approach isn't working well.

Perhaps you have a group of young leaders that need to be pushed, challenged, and stretched. Draw from your bucket of gas, light a fire under them. They are too comfortable and need to grow. Placing them in roles with increased responsibilities will be a good thing. Get them out of their comfort zone and see what they are capable of. If you don't they will get complacent, become disengaged, and not reach their full potential. It is amazing what even just a little heat can do to get people moving with urgency.

If you are swamped and so busy you have lost connection with your staff, slow down, walk slowly through the halls and visit with people. Sometimes you have been running too hot and need some water to recover. Staying connected to people relationally can be a source of refreshment. When you get out of the office and spend time with people, you gain a clearer perspective on what is actually going on with others. Encouraging people and providing a listening ear will help you gain discernment on how to proceed. Some people may be struggling in their personal life. There might be some office conflict you haven't been aware of that needs attending. Maybe the economy is hitting hard and inflation is crushing everyone's pockets, or someone needs to vent and share their frustrations with you to see if you care. Each scenario can be so different but at the end of the day, you will utilize one of the buckets. There isn't a right or wrong bucket to use. What you choose, and how you choose to use each bucket will decide your outcome. That is the beauty and power of being a leader. Some of you are just starting out and learning how to lead. You will make mistakes as you go, but learn from them. Try different approaches and styles. See what works for you and adjust as you go. Be flexible. What worked in one position may not work in another.

Avoid trying to always find an absolute. Leadership is lived in the gray areas. There can be great times of uncertainty when leading and it is during those times you need to be open to different approaches and techniques. That is why the two buckets are so powerful. Water can cool, refresh, cleanse, dampen and drown. Gas can empower, fuel, energize, or cause damage and burn up. Use each bucket wisely and use them often. You and your people need it and your leadership depends on it.

ENDNOTES

1   Tolan, T. (2013, June 24). *Where are you on the sigmoid curve?*. Healthcare Innovation.https://www. hcinnovationgroup.com/finance-revenue-cycle/blog/13017457/ where-are-you-on-the-sigmoid-curve

2   *Do it anyway - mother teresa.* Mother Teresa - Do it Anyway (wise living). (n.d.). https://www.asa3.org/ASA/education/views/ teresa.htm

3   Taieb, M. (2017, July 22). *Be the change you want to see in the world.* Medium. https://medium.com/@LibyanRunner/ be-the-change-you-want-to-see-in-the-world-66ca95186c99

4   Baker, / Denis. (2020, January 1). *Fool.* LEADER INFLUENCE. https://leaderinfluence.net/tag/fool/

5   *Breaking the sound barrier: Chuck Yeager and the Bell X-1.* Homepage. (n.d.). https://airandspace.si.edu/stories/editorial/ breaking-sound-barrier-75th

6   *"make no small plans for they have no power to stir the soul." -Niccolo Machiavelli.* The Foundation for a Better Life. (n.d.). https://www.passiton.com/inspirational-quotes/4386-make-no-small-plans-for-they-have-no-power-to

7   Catmull, E., & Wallace, A. (2023). *Creativity, Inc.: Overcoming the unseen forces that stand in the way of true inspiration.* Random House Canada.

8   *John C. Maxwell quote.* A. (n.d.). https://www.azquotes.com/quote/1215327

9   Habakkuk 2:2 NKJV - - bible gateway. (n.d.). https://www.biblegateway.com/passage/?search=Habakkuk%2B2%3A2&version=NKJV

10   Stanley, A. (2009). *Making Vision Stick.* Zondervan.

11   *Nathan Armstrong quote: "if you fail to plan, you're planning to fail." – Benjamin Franklin.".* Quotefancy. (n.d.). https://quotefancy.com/quote/2576665/Nathan-Armstrong-If-you-fail-to-plan-you-re-planning-to-fail-Benjamin-Franklin

12   Stanley, A. (2017). In *Going deep & wide: A companion guide for churches and leaders* (p. 159). essay, Zondervan.

13   Davey Blackburn. (2019, August 13). *Run toward the Roar.* https://www.daveyblackburn.com/blog/run-toward-the-roar

14   *Survey reveals impact of lack of employee appreciation at work: Blueboard blog.* RSS. (n.d.). https://www.blueboard.com/blog/survey-reveals-appreciation-improves-employee-engagement#:~:text=A%20survey%20of%20400%20employed,a%20strong%20culture%20of%20appreciation.

15   *Maya Angelou quote: "People will forget what you said, people will forget what you did, but people will never forget how you made them feel."* Quotefancy. (n.d.-a). https://quotefancy.com/quote/31/Maya-Angelou-People-will-forget-what-you-said-people-will-forget-what-you-did-but-people

16   *John C. Maxwell quote: "Leaders touch a heart before they ask for a hand."* Quotefancy. (n.d.-a). https://quotefancy.com/quote/841244/John-C-Maxwell-Leaders-touch-a-heart-before-they-ask-for-a-hand

17   Gratitude may be the secret to overcoming the talent crisis - fast company. (n.d.). https://www.fastcompany.com/90665927/gratitude-may-be-the-secret-to-overcoming-the-talent-crisis

18   Tice, L. E., & Quick, J. (2004). *Personal coaching for results: How to mentor and inspire others to amazing growth.* Thomas Nelson Publishers, a division of Thomas Nelson, Inc.

19   Heath, C., & Heath, D. (2019). *The power of moments: Why certain experiences have extraordinary impact.* Corgi.

20   *Maimonides quote: "give a man a fish and you feed him for a day; teach a man to fish and you feed him for a lifetime."* Quotefancy. (n.d.-b). https://quotefancy.com/quote/1308687/Maimonides-Give-a-man-a-fish-and-you-feed-him-for-a-day-teach-a-man-to-fish-and-you-feed

21   *Tony Robbins quote: "repetition is the mother of skill."* Quotefancy. (n.d.-f). https://quotefancy.com/quote/922729/Tony-Robbins-Repetition-is-the-mother-of-skill

22   *Paths, levels and electives.* Toastmasters International -Pathways Leadership Development Path. (n.d.). https://www.toastmasters.org/pathways-overview/pathways-leadership-development-path

23   Goodwin, D. K. (2006). *Team of rivals: The political genius of Abraham Lincoln.* Simon & Schuster Paperbacks.

24   *How diversity can drive innovation.* Harvard Business Review. (2014, August 1). https://hbr.org/2013/12/how-diversity-can-drive-innovation

25   McChrystal, S. (2015). *Team of teams: New rules of engagement for a complex world.* Portfolio Penguin.

26   Sinek, S. (2017). *Leaders eat last.* Portfolio Penguin.

27   Maxwell, J. C. (2008). *Leadership gold.* Thomas Nelson.

28   *John C. Maxwell quote: "anyone can steer a ship, but it takes a leader to chart the course."* Quotefancy. (n.d.-a). https://quotefancy.com/quote/841047/John-C-Maxwell-Anyone-can-steer-a-ship-but-it-takes-a-leader-to-chart-the-course

29   (1961, February 1). *What species of Eagle pushes their young to teach them flying?.* Biology Stack Exchange. https://biology.stackexchange.com/questions/26361/what-species-of-eagle-pushes-their-young-to-teach-them-flying

30   Renner, B. (2022, December 12). *Survey: It takes americans 4 days to stop thinking about work while on vacation.* Study Finds. https://studyfinds.org/american-need-four-days-stop-thinking-about-work-vacation/

31   *Breaks are the key to high productivity.* Business News Daily. (n.d.). https://www.businessnewsdaily.com/6387-employee-breaks.html

32   Grant, A. (2013). *Give and take.* Weidenfeld and Nicolson.

33   Sweet, L. I., & Hammett, E. H. (2007). *The gospel according to Starbucks: Living with a grande passion.* Waterbrook Press.

34   Ware, B. (2019). *Top Five regrets of the dying: A life transformed by the dearly departing, the.* Hay House Inc.

35   *Rhein Fathia quote: "sometimes, 'someday' means 'I know it will never happen'."* Quotefancy. (n.d.-e). https://quotefancy.com/quote/2834716/Rhein-Fathia-Sometimes-someday-means-I-know-it-will-never-happen

36   John Maxwell. (2014, April 25). *A new definition of success.* https://www.johnmaxwell.com/blog/a-new-definition-of-success/

37   Curran, E. J. (2023, February 13). *7 unexpected benefits of eating together as a family, according to science.* Parents. https://www.parents.com/recipes/tips/unexpected-benefits-of-eating-together-as-a-family-according-to-science/

ACKNOWLEDGEMENTS

I would like to start off by thanking and honoring my dad and mom. Though they are no longer with me, their love, support, and guidance through the years helped me grow up and be the best husband and father I could be.

I would also like to thank all of the mentors, coaches, and athletes through the years I have had the privilege of learning from and working with. Without them, I wouldn't have made it this far and learned all the valuable lessons that have sustained me in my career. I stand upon your shoulders.

Specifically, at the University of Texas there have been so many people I am grateful for. Coach Mack Brown and Jeff "Maddog" Madden for hiring me in 1998, DeLoss Dodds and Chris Plonsky for their leadership, support, example and encouragement, Chris Del Conte who has taught me no goal is too big, Coach Jerritt Elliott who taught me that good people love people, Coach Michael Center who has taught me how to rebuild your life when it comes crashing down, Coach Bruce Berque who has taught me the importance of details and organization to be successful, and Allen "Godfather" Hardin who has been in my corner from day one encouraging me and helping grow as a leader.

I would also like to say a special thanks to all the staff I have had the privilege of working alongside with and serving through the years at Texas. Sandy Abney, Trey Zepeda, Anna Craig, Melissa Schmtiz, Clint Martin, Michael Hanson, Joe Krawczyk, Matt Couch, Nic Higgins, Jesse Ackerman, Tim Cross, Derrick Scott, Chuck Faucette, Jeff Earls, Angel Spassov, Lee McCormick, Stephen Whalen, Lance Sewell, Beth Byron, and Brent Metz. Thank you for all the memories, lessons, and support.

I would also like to specially thank some mentors who have significantly impacted my life and career trajectory. Coach Steve Duke, my high school offensive line coach who pushed me to greatness and to this day still calls me "stud". E. J. "Doc" Kreis who sadly passed away recently but if it weren't for him, I wouldn't be where I am today as a coach and leader. Thank you Doc! He not only coached me in his free time when I was struggling as a college athlete at Georgia, he gave me my first job to coach at the University of Colorado when I had no idea of what my career would be. Dave Plettl, a true friend, mentor, and colleague that has always been a great example of what it means to coach with excellence and not neglect your family along the way. Coach Dan Pfaff, who was the first coach and mentor to teach how to analyze the body and movement from a global perspective. To Jim Tindall, my karate instructor who would teach and train me one on one in his spare time. I learned more about life in our talks after class than how to defend myself. To my pastor, Dave Jamerson who has selflessly encouraged me, believed in me, giving me opportunities to grow as a communicator and leader, prayed for me, and pushed me into all God has for me.

I would also like to say thank you to my editor, Thelma Nienhuis who has helped turn this dream into a reality. Your feedback, guidance and coaching has helped me to do the impossible. To Taryn Nergaard and the team at Typewriter Creative. There is no way I could complete this project without you and your team bringing it to life.

Most importantly I want to say thank you to my family. To my amazing, beautiful, encouraging, sacrificial, and supportive wife Karen. You have put up with all my crazy dreams and believed in me when I didn't believe in myself. Your words of wisdom and insight are all throughout the pages of this book. To my four beautiful, talented, courageous daughters: Isabel, Anna, Evelyn, and Olivia. The love you have given me and the lessons you have taught me from the moment I laid eyes on you have been the difference maker in my life. You guys are my "why"! Thank you for being so patient, gracious and forgiving to a hard headed and stubborn dad that still needs to be told when to get a haircut. I couldn't have prayed for or been more proud of the young women you are growing up to be. You guys are true leaders! I know you will go further and higher in life than I could ever dreamed of.

DONNIE MAIB

Director of Olympic Sports Athletic Performance

University of Texas

Coach Donnie Maib is in his 31st year as a Strength and Conditioning Coach. He began his coaching career at the University of Colorado in 1994 where he worked with E. J. "Doc" Kreis until 1997. Coach Maib trained all varsity teams while at Colorado, where he helped many athletes obtain All-Conference as well as All-American accolades.

From 1998 until the present, Coach Maib has been at the University of Texas, where he is currently the Head Coach for Athletic Performance (Olympic Sports). As a director at Texas, Coach Maib oversees and manages 8 other performance staff and oversees 4 weight rooms. In his tenure at Texas, Coach Maib has worked with a variety of sports including Football, Women's Track, Men's and Women's Golf, Women's Soccer, Men's Tennis, and Women's Volleyball.

Most recently, Volleyball won the 2022 and 2023 National Championship and Men's Tennis won the 2019 National Championship. Volleyball has been Big XII conference champions in 2007, 2008, 2009, 2011, 2012, 2013, 2014, 2015, 2017, 2018, 2019, 2020, 2021, 2022, and 2023. In 2006, 2008, 2010, 2014, 2018, 2019, 2021, 2023 and 2024 the Men's Tennis team won the Big XII conference championship. In 2005, with Coach Maib's assistance, the University of Texas football team won the National Championship in the Rose Bowl. Additionally, under his direct supervision, Women's Track won National Championships in both their indoor and outdoor seasons in 1999. Coach Maib has had the privilege of coaching numerous Olympians, All-Conference, as well as All-American athletes, at the University of Texas. In football alone, while working alongside Coach Madden and Coach Mack Brown, there have been over 30 players drafted into the NFL in the past during his coaching era.

Coach Maib holds a 1st degree black belt in Kenpo Karate and has authored two prior books: *Speed-Strength Training for Martial Artists* and *The Secret Sauce of Leadership.* In addition to his coaching responsibilities, Donnie started the 1st Athletic Performance Coaches Clinic for the University of Texas Athletics that brings in some of the most elite Coaches in the country to present on current topics and trends in the strength and conditioning industry. In 2020,

Coach Maib launched The Team Behind the Team podcast. It is a unique and first of its kind collegiate athletics show that focuses on bringing world class experts and education on the topics of athletic performance, sports medicine, performance nutrition, sports science and mental health and wellness.

Coach Maib played football at Gallatin Senior High School where he earned All-State, All-Decade, and All-American Honors. He went on to earn a full scholarship at the University of Georgia where he lettered and started for 3 years at defensive tackle.

Donnie has been married 28 years to his wonderful wife Karen and they have four beautiful daughters: Isabel, Anna, Evelyn, and Olivia.